Accumula 7
STUDENT BOOK

JUMP Math
One Yonge Street, Suite 1014
Toronto, Ontario M5E 1E5
Canada
www.jumpmath.org

Writers: Dr. Sohrab Rahbar, Dr. Sindi Sabourin
Editors: Megan Burns, Liane Tsui, Natalie Francis, Dishpreet Kaur, Janice Dyer, Wendy Scavuzzo, Joe Zingrone
Layout and Illustrations: Linh Lam, Sawyer Paul, Gabriella Kerr, Marijke Friesen, Pam Lostracco
Cover Design: Sunday Lek
Cover Photograph: © ONiONA/Shutterstock

ISBN 978-1-77395-299-4

First printing January 2024

Parts of this material were first published in 2015 in AP Book 7.1, US edition (978-1-927457-47-4) and AP Book 7.2, US edition (978-1-927457-48-1).

Printed and bound in Canada

Welcome to JUMP Math!

Entering the world of JUMP Math means believing that every learner has the capacity to be fully numerate and love math.

The **JUMP Math Accumula Student Book** is the companion to the **JUMP Math Accumula** supplementary resource for Grades 1 to 8, which is designed to strengthen foundational math knowledge and prepare all students for success in understanding math problems at grade level. This book provides opportunities for students to consolidate learning by exploring important math concepts through independent practice.

Unique Evidence-Based Approach and Resources

JUMP Math's unique approach, Kindergarten to Grade 8 resources, and professional learning for teachers have been producing positive learning outcomes for children and teachers in classrooms in Canada, the United States, and other countries for over 20 years. Our resources are aligned with the science on how children's brains learn best and have been demonstrated through studies to greatly improve problem solving, computation, and fluency skills. (See our research at **jumpmath.org**.) Our approach is designed to build equity by supporting the full spectrum of learners to achieve success in math.

Confidence Building is Key

JUMP Math begins each grade with review to enable every student to quickly develop the confidence needed to engage deeply with math. Our distinctive incremental approach to learning math concepts gradually increases the level of difficulty for students, empowering them to become motivated, independent problem solvers. Our books are also designed with simple pictures and models to avoid overwhelming learners when introducing new concepts, enabling them to see the deep structure of the math and gain the confidence to solve a wide range of math problems.

About JUMP Math

JUMP Math is a non-profit organization dedicated to helping every child in every classroom develop confidence, understanding, and a love of math. JUMP Math also offers a comprehensive set of classroom resources for students in Kindergarten to Grade 8.

For more information, visit JUMP Math at: www.jumpmath.org.

Contents

1. Patterns

1. Find the number that was added or subtracted each time. Then extend the pattern.

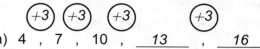

a) 4 , 7 , 10 , _13_ , _16_

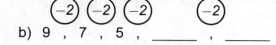

b) 9 , 7 , 5 , _____ , _____

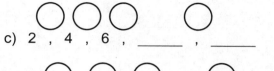

c) 2 , 4 , 6 , _____ , _____

d) 11 , 7 , 3 , _____ , _____

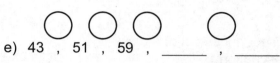

e) 43 , 51 , 59 , _____ , _____

f) 82 , 74 , 66 , _____ , _____

> If you know the **rule** for a sequence, you can create the sequence.
>
> Examples: The rule is: Start at 2 and add 3 each time. The sequence is: 2, 5, 8, 11, …
>
> The rule is: 2, 7, 1, then repeat. The sequence is: 2, 7, 1, 2, 7, 1, …

2. State the rule for the sequence.

a) 22, 27, 32, 37   The rule is: _____

b) 49, 46, 43, 40   The rule is: _____

c) 8, 4, 8, 4, 8, 4   The rule is: _____

d) 85, 81, 77, 73   The rule is: _____

3. Create the sequence from the rule.

a) Start at 7 and add 5 each time. _____, _____, _____, _____

b) Start at 45 and subtract 4 each time. _____, _____, _____, _____

c) 0, 6, then repeat. _____, _____, _____, _____

4. Does the sequence **increase** (go up), **decrease** (go down), or **repeat**?

a) 2, 4, 8, 16, 32, 64 _____   b) 3, 7, 1, 3, 7, 1 _____

c) 29, 27, 25, 23, 21 _____   d) 2, 6, 10, 14, 18 _____

e) 11, 9, 6, 11, 9, 6 _____   f) 61, 56, 51, 46, 41 _____

5. A marina rents sailboats at a rate of $8 for the first hour and $5 for every hour after that. How much does it cost to rent a sailboat from the marina for 4 hours?

6. Rani has a roll of 85 stamps. She uses 9 each day for 4 days. How many are left?

7. Match each sequence with the correct description (**A**, **B**, or **C**).

a)   **A.** increases by 5 each time
    B. increases by different amounts
    C. repeats

    8, 12, 18, 22, 24, 28 _____

    7, 12, 12 , 7, 12, 12 _____

    7, 12, 17, 22, 27, 32 _____

b)   **A.** increases and decreases
    B. decreases by different amounts
    C. decreases by the same amount

    18, 16, 14, 12, 10 _____

    31, 29, 25, 13, 9 _____

    6, 9, 14, 10, 5 _____

8. Make 3 sequences that match the descriptions. Write the sequences out of order. Ask a partner to match each sequence with the correct description.

    A. increases by 4 each time   _____ _____

    B. increases by different amounts   _____ _____

    C. increases and decreases   _____ _____

9. a) Find the numbers that were added. Then extend the pattern.

    1 , 1 , 2 , 3 , 5 , 8 , 13 , 21 , 34 , _____, _____, _____

  b) The sequence in part a) is called the **Fibonacci sequence**. How can you get each term in the sequence from the previous two terms?

    _____

  c) Complete the table by writing "E" for even and "O" for odd.

Number	1	1	2	3	5	8	13	21	34
Even or Odd?									

    Write the rule for the even-odd pattern in the Fibonacci sequence.

    _____

10. Find the gaps between the gaps and extend the patterns.

    (+3)
    (+2) (+5)
    1 , 3 , 8 , 17 , 31 , 51 , _____, _____, _____

Bonus ▶ Find the gaps and extend the pattern.

    10 , 11 , 9 , 12 , 8 , 13 , _____, _____, _____

2. T-tables

Tom creates an **increasing pattern** with squares.

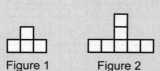
Figure 1

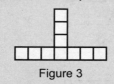
Figure 2

Figure 3

Figure	Number of Squares
1	4
2	7
3	10

The number of squares in the figures are 4, 7, 10, ...

Tom writes a rule for the number of squares: Start at 4 and add 3 each time.

1. Tom makes other increasing patterns with squares. How many squares does he add to make each new figure?

   Write your answers in the circles. Then write a rule for the pattern.

a)

Figure	Number of Squares
1	2
2	7
3	12
4	17

Rule:

_____

_____

b)

Figure	Number of Squares
1	6
2	14
3	22
4	30

Rule:

_____

_____

c)

Figure	Number of Squares
1	12
2	25
3	38
4	51

Rule:

_____

_____

2. Use a T-table to find out how many toothpicks will be required to make the fifth figure in each pattern.

   a)

   b)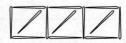

3. Wang has $79 and spends $3 per week. Kam has $84 and spends $4 per week. How many weeks will it take for them to have the same amount of money left?

Bonus ▶

a) Draw a T-table to predict the number of shaded parts in Figure 5 of this pattern.

Figure 1

Figure 2

Figure 3

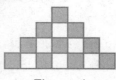
Figure 4

b) Will the number of shaded parts in Figure 15 be even or odd?

4. Extend the columns. What is the rule for how you get the numbers in the second column from the first column?

a)

Add 10	Add 10
2	5
12	
22	
32	

_____

b)

Add 4	Add 4
7	3

_____

c)

Subtract 2	Subtract 2
38	45

_____

5. Maria continues two sequences for the same number of steps:

   Start at 4 and add 13.   Start at 9 and add 13.

   When the first sequence reaches 251, what number will the second sequence reach? _____

6. Marco had $35 and Ava had $40. Then, they both started earning $17 an hour for mowing their friends' lawns. When Ava has $210, how much money will Marco have?

7. Extend the columns. What is the rule for how you get the numbers in the second column from the first column?

a)

Multiply by 2	Multiply by 2
2	6

_____

b)

Divide by 3	Divide by 3
9	18

_____

c)

Multiply by 10	Multiply by 10
6	3

_____

8. Josh continues two sequences for the same number of steps:

   Start at 9 and multiply by 8   Start at 90 and multiply by 8.

   When the first sequence reaches 36,864, what number will the second sequence reach? _____

9. Yu had $96 when Raj had $160. They both spend half their money every week.

   When Yu has $12 left, how much money will Raj have left? _____

3. Lowest Common Multiples

The whole numbers are the numbers 0, 1, 2, 3, and so on.

The **multiples** of a whole number are the numbers you get by multiplying the number by another whole number.

Examples: $2 \times 3 = 6$, so 6 is a multiple of both 2 and 3.
$0 \times 5 = 0$, so 0 is a multiple of both 0 and 5.

1. a) Skip count to write the multiples of 3 up to 3×10.

   ___0___, ___3___, _____, _____, _____, _____, _____, _____, _____, _____, _____

   b) Use your answers in part a) to circle the multiples of 3.

   12   17   22   24   25   27

2. Mark the multiples of each number on the number lines.

2: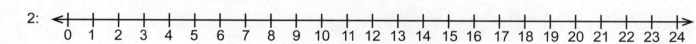

3: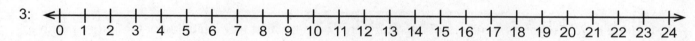

4: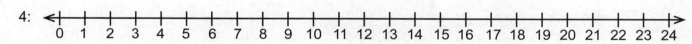

5:

6: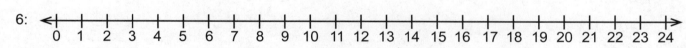

A number is a **common multiple** of two numbers if it is a multiple of both of them.

3. Find the first 2 common multiples (after 0) of …

   a) 2 and 5: _____, _____   b) 3 and 6: _____, _____   c) 2 and 4: _____, _____

   d) 3 and 4: _____, _____   e) 4 and 6: _____, _____   f) 2 and 6: _____, _____

4. a) How can you find the second common multiple of two numbers from the first?

   b) The first common multiple of 18 and 42 is 126. What is the second common multiple?

5. a) Write the first 4 common multiples of 2 and 3, after 0. _____, _____, _____, _____

   b) Extend the pattern from part a). Predict the fifth common multiple of 2 and 3. _____

The number 0 is a multiple of every number. The **lowest common multiple** (**LCM**) of two numbers is the smallest whole number (not 0) that is a multiple of both of them.

The common multiples of two numbers are the multiples of the LCM.

6. Find the lowest common multiple of each pair of numbers.

a) 4 and 10

4: *4, 8, 12, 16, 20*

10: *10, 20*

LCM = _____

b) 3 and 6

3:

6:

LCM = _____

c) 8 and 10

8:

10:

LCM = _____

d) 6 and 8

6:

8:

LCM = _____

To find the lowest common multiple of two numbers, write the first few multiples of the larger number until you see one that is also a multiple of the smaller number.

Example: Find the LCM of 3 and 5.
        The first few multiples of 5 are 5, 10, and 15. Stop here because 15 is a multiple of 3.

7. Find the LCM.

a) 6 and 10

10, 20, 30

LCM = ___30___

b) 9 and 12

LCM = _____

c) 7 and 10

LCM = _____

d) 6 and 30

LCM = _____

e) 6 and 15

LCM = _____

f) 8 and 9

LCM = _____

g) 5 and 8

LCM = _____

h) 6 and 9

LCM = _____

4. Comparing Fractions Using Equivalent Fractions

Two or more fractions are equivalent if they can be shown by the same part of the same whole.

Example: $\frac{2}{3}$ and $\frac{4}{6}$ are equivalent fractions.

$\frac{2}{3} =$

1. What equivalent fractions do these pictures show?

$\frac{1}{2}$ = _____ = _____ = _____

2. Shade the same part to find a fraction equivalent to the first fraction.

a)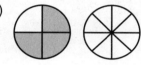

$\frac{3}{4}$ = _____

b)

$\frac{1}{3}$ = _____

c)

$\frac{3}{5}$ = _____

3. Fill in the blanks.

a) A has _____ times as many parts as B.

   A has _____ times as many shaded parts as B.

b) A has _____ times as many parts as B.

   A has _____ times as many shaded parts as B.

4. Compare the numerators and denominators by multiplication.

a) $\frac{1}{4}$ and $\frac{2}{8}$

2 is _____ times as much as 1.

8 is _____ times as much as 4.

b)  $\frac{4}{5}$ and $\frac{12}{15}$

12 is _____ times as much as 4.

15 is _____ times as much as 5.

You can multiply the numerator and denominator by the same number to get an equivalent fraction.

Example: A   B

$$\frac{3}{4} \xrightarrow[\times 2]{\times 2} = \frac{6}{8}$$

B has twice as many **parts** as A.
B has twice as many **shaded parts** as A.

5. Draw lines to cut the pies into more pieces. Then fill in the numerators of the equivalent fractions.

a)

                                  $\frac{1}{2} = \frac{}{4} = \frac{}{6} = \frac{}{8}$

  4 pieces   6 pieces   8 pieces

b)

                                    $\frac{1}{3} = \frac{}{6} = \frac{}{9} = \frac{}{12}$

  6 pieces   9 pieces   12 pieces

6. Cut each pie into more pieces. Then fill in the missing numbers.

a) 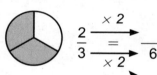 $\frac{2}{3} \xrightarrow[\times 2]{\times 2} = \frac{}{6}$
    b) 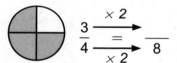 $\frac{3}{4} \xrightarrow[\times 2]{\times 2} = \frac{}{8}$
    c) 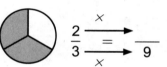 $\frac{2}{3} \xrightarrow[\times]{\times} = \frac{}{9}$

                       This number tells you how many pieces to cut each slice into.

7. Use multiplication to find the equivalent fraction.

a) $\dfrac{1 \times 2}{3 \times 2} = \dfrac{}{6}$
          b) $\dfrac{1 \times}{2 \times} = \dfrac{}{10}$
          c) $\dfrac{4}{5} = \dfrac{}{10}$

d) $\dfrac{3}{4} = \dfrac{}{8}$
          e) $\dfrac{1}{3} = \dfrac{}{12}$
          f) $\dfrac{4}{5} = \dfrac{}{25}$

g) $\dfrac{7}{8} = \dfrac{}{16}$
          h) $\dfrac{9}{10} = \dfrac{}{100}$
          i) $\dfrac{2}{9} = \dfrac{}{72}$

8. Write five fractions equivalent to $\dfrac{3}{10}$.

$$\frac{3}{10} = \boxed{} = \boxed{} = \boxed{} = \boxed{} = \boxed{}$$

JUMP Math Accumula

9. Shade the fractions provided. Then order the fractions from least to greatest.

$\frac{3}{5}$ $\frac{1}{5}$ $\frac{4}{5}$ ⊘ $\frac{2}{5}$ ⊘
☐ < ☐ < ☐ < ☐

10. Two fractions have the same denominators (bottoms) but different numerators (tops). How can you tell which fraction is greater?

_____

11. Circle the greater fraction in each pair.

a) $\frac{1}{8}$ or $\frac{3}{8}$

b) $\frac{4}{9}$ or $\frac{2}{9}$

c) $\frac{5}{11}$ or $\frac{8}{11}$

d) $\frac{9}{31}$ or $\frac{6}{31}$

12. a) Write an equivalent fraction with denominator 12.

i) $\frac{2}{3} = \frac{\quad}{12}$

ii) $\frac{5}{6} = \frac{\quad}{12}$

iii) $\frac{3}{4} = \frac{\quad}{12}$

iv) $\frac{1}{2} = \frac{\quad}{12}$

b) Write the original fractions from part a) in order from least to greatest.

☐ < ☐ < ☐ < ☐

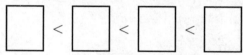

Pedro wants to compare $\frac{3}{4}$ and $\frac{5}{6}$. He turns them into fractions with the same denominator.

$\frac{3 \times 6}{4 \times 6} = \frac{18}{24}$ and $\frac{5 \times 4}{6 \times 4} = \frac{20}{24}$, so $\frac{3}{4} < \frac{5}{6}$.

13. Turn the fractions into fractions with the same denominator. Then compare the fractions. Show your answer using < or >.

a) $\frac{5}{7} = \frac{\quad}{28}$ and $\frac{3}{4} = \frac{\quad}{28}$

so $\frac{5}{7}$ ☐ $\frac{3}{4}$.

b) $\frac{5}{7} = \frac{\quad}{\quad}$ and $\frac{7}{10} = \frac{\quad}{\quad}$

so $\frac{5}{7}$ ☐ $\frac{7}{10}$.

c) $\frac{1}{2} = \frac{\quad}{\quad}$ and $\frac{3}{4} = \frac{\quad}{\quad}$

so $\frac{1}{2}$ ☐ $\frac{3}{4}$.

14. Compare $\frac{5}{6}$ and $\frac{7}{8}$ by using the smallest common denominator that you can.

The LCM of 6 and 8 is _____, so use _____ as the common denominator.

$\frac{5}{6} = \frac{\quad}{\quad}$ and $\frac{7}{8} = \frac{\quad}{\quad}$, so $\frac{5}{6}$ ☐ $\frac{7}{8}$.

15. In the grey box above, what smaller denominator could Pedro use to compare $\frac{3}{4}$ and $\frac{5}{6}$? _____

5. Fractions and Ratios

> A fraction compares a part to a whole. A **ratio** can compare a part to a part, or a part to a whole.
>
> Example: ○ ○ □ □ ○
>
>   The **part-to-part ratio** of circles to squares is 3 to 2 or 3 : 2.
>
>   The **part-to-whole ratio** of circles to shapes is 3 to 5 or 3 : 5.

1. ☆ ☾ ○ □ □ ○ ○ ○ □ ☆ △ ○ ☆ ○ ☾ □

   a) The ratio of moons to circles is _____ : _____. b) The ratio of triangles to moons is _____ : _____.

   c) The ratio of stars to squares is _____ : _____. d) The ratio of triangles to shapes is _____ : _____.

2. Build a model or draw a picture that could be described by the ratio 3 : 4.

3. a) Write the ratio of vowels (a, e, i, o, u) to consonants (other letters) in the word.

      i) star   _____ : _____   ii) moon   _____ : _____

      iii) circle   _____ : _____   iv) square   _____ : _____

      v) triangle   _____ : _____

   b) Are the ratios you found in part a) part-to-part ratios or part-to-whole ratios?

      _____

4. Circle the part-to-whole ratios. Underline the part-to-part ratios.

   a) vowels in "band" : letters in "band"   b) vowels in "blog" : consonants in "blog"

   c) buses : trucks   d) school buses to buses

   e) school days to days of the week   f) days in January to days in September

5. Write the ratio of the lengths.

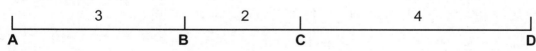

   a) AB to CD = _____ : _____   b) BC to CD = _____ : _____

   c) AB to AC = _____ : _____   d) CD to AD = _____ : _____

6. Which ratios from Question 5 are part-to-whole ratios? _____

A part-to-whole ratio can be thought of as a fraction.

Example: ◯◯△△△

The ratio of circles to shapes is 2 to 5 or 2 : 5, so $\frac{2}{5}$ of the shapes are circles.

7. Write a ratio and a fraction.

a) ◯◯◯△△△△

circles to shapes = _____ : _____

_____ of the shapes are circles.

b) ◯◯△△△△△

circles to shapes = _____ : _____

_____ of the shapes are circles.

A part-to-part ratio can sometimes be changed to a fraction.

Example: There are 3 circles for every 5 triangles in a set of circles and triangles.

◯◯◯△△△△△

There are 3 circles for every 8 shapes, so $\frac{3}{8}$ of the shapes are circles.

8. Write the number of boys (b), girls (g), and students (s) in each class.

a) There are 8 boys and 5 girls in a class.   b: __8__   g: __5__   s: __13__

b) There are 9 girls in a class of 20 students.   b: _____   g: _____   s: _____

c) There are 3 boys in a class of 10 students.   b: _____   g: _____   s: _____

9. Write the fraction of students in the class who are boys and the fraction who are girls.

a) There are 5 boys and 8 girls in the class.   b: ☐   g: ☐

b) The ratio of boys to girls in the class is 5 to 9.   b: ☐   g: ☐

c) The ratio of girls to boys in the class is 6 : 7.   b: ☐   g: ☐

10. In Mr. X's class, $\frac{2}{5}$ of the students are girls. In Ms. Y's class, $\frac{5}{8}$ of the students are girls.

a) What is the ratio of girls to boys in each class?   Mr. X's class   Ms. Y's class

= _____ : _____   = _____ : _____

b) Whose class has more girls than boys? How can you tell from the fraction? How can you tell from the ratio?

6. Equivalent Ratios

In the picture, there are 3 circles for every 2 squares.
There are also 6 circles for every 4 squares.

The ratios 3 : 2 and 6 : 4 are **equivalent**.

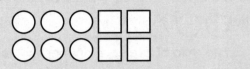

1. Find two equivalent ratios for each picture.

   a)

   circles to squares = 3 : _____ = 6: _____

   b)

   circles to squares = 1 : _____ = 2 : _____

   c)

   circles to squares = 2 : _____ = 6: _____

   d)

   circles to squares = 3 : _____ = 9 : _____

2. Complete the pictures so the ratio of triangles to squares is the same in each column. Then create a sequence of equivalent ratios.

Triangles	△△	△△ △△	
Squares	□□□		□□□ □□□ □□□
Ratio	2 : 3		

Triangles	△△△	△△△ △△△	
Squares		□ □	□ □ □
Ratio		6 : 2	

3. Skip count to write a sequence of three equivalent ratios.

   a) 3 : 2 = _6_ : _4_ = ____ : ____

   b) 3 : 5 = ____ : ____ = ____ : ____

   c) 5 : 8 = ____ : ____ = ____ : ____

   d) 3 : 10 = ____ : ____ = ____ : ____

   e) 5 : 4 = ____ : ____ = ____ : ____

   f) 4 : 9 = ____ : ____ = ____ : ____

4. Skip count to write a sequence of five equivalent ratios.

   4 : 3 = ____ : ____ = ____ : ____ = ____ : ____ = ____ : ____

There are 5 girls for every 2 boys in a class. There are 20 girls.

To find out how many boys are in the class, write out a
sequence of equivalent ratios. Stop when there are 20 girls.

There are 8 boys in the class.

Girls		Boys
5	:	2
10	:	4
15	:	6
20	:	8

5. Write a sequence of equivalent ratios to solve each problem.

a) There are 5 boys for every 4 girls in a class with 20 boys.   **Boys   Girls**
    How many girls are in the class?

b) There are 4 red beads for every 3 blue beads in a bracelet.   **Red   Blue**
    The bracelet has 12 red beads. How many blue beads
    are in the bracelet?

c) A recipe for soup calls for 3 cups of cream for every   **Cream   Tomatoes**
    5 cups of tomatoes. How many cups of cream are
    needed for 15 cups of tomatoes?

d) A team has 2 wins for every loss. They won 10 games.   **Wins   Losses**
    How many games did they lose?

e) A mixture for green paint has 5 cups of blue paint for every 6 cups of yellow paint.
    How much blue paint would you need if you have 30 cups of yellow paint?

There are 3 boys for every 2 girls in a class of 20 students.

To find out how many boys are in the class, write out a sequence of equivalent ratios. Stop when the terms add to 20.

12 boys + 8 girls = 20 students, so there are 12 boys in the class.

Boys		Girls	Total
3	:	2	5
6	:	4	10
9	:	6	15
12	:	8	20

6. Write a sequence of equivalent ratios to solve each problem.

a) There are 5 boys for every 4 girls in a class of 27 students. How many girls are in the class?

Boys   Girls   Total

b) There are 2 red marbles for every 7 blue marbles in a box. If the box has 45 marbles, how many marbles are blue?

Red   Blue   Total

c) A recipe for punch calls for 3 cups of orange juice for every 4 cups of mango juice. How many cups of orange juice are needed to make 21 cups of punch?

Orange   Mango   Total

d) A team has 5 wins for every 2 losses. They played 35 games. How many games did they lose?

Wins   Losses   Total

e) A mixture for green paint has 2 cups of blue paint for every 3 cups of yellow paint. How much blue paint would you need to make 20 cups of green paint?

7. Ratio Tables

To create an equivalent ratio, multiply each term in the ratio by the same number.

Example: Draw 2 circles and 1 square four times.

There are now 2 × 4 circles and 1 × 4 squares. So the ratio of circles to squares is:

$$\times 4$$
$$2 : 1 = 8 : 4$$
$$\times 4$$

1. What number are both terms being multiplied by to make the second ratio?

a) $\times \underline{\quad}$
   $1 : 3 = 4 : 12$

b) $\times \underline{\quad}$
   $2 : 5 = 6 : 15$

c) $\times \underline{\quad}$
   $3 : 4 = 18 : 24$

d) $\times \underline{\quad}$
   $3 : 5 = 12 : 20$

e) $\times \underline{\quad}$
   $2 : 3 = 6 : 9$

f) $\times \underline{\quad}$
   $1 : 4 = 13 : 52$

2. Multiply both terms by the same number to make an equivalent ratio.

a) $\times 4 \left(\begin{array}{c} 2 : 3 \end{array} \right) \times \underline{\quad}$
   $\underline{\quad} : \underline{\quad}$

b) $\times 5 \left(\begin{array}{c} 2 : 5 \end{array} \right) \times \underline{\quad}$
   $\underline{\quad} : \underline{\quad}$

c) $\times 5 \left(\begin{array}{c} 3 : 4 \end{array} \right) \times \underline{\quad}$
   $\underline{\quad} : \underline{\quad}$

d) $\times \underline{\quad} \left(\begin{array}{c} 4 : 5 \end{array} \right) \times 3$
   $\underline{\quad} : \underline{\quad}$

e) $\times \underline{\quad} \left(\begin{array}{c} 2 : 7 \end{array} \right) \times 4$
   $\underline{\quad} : \underline{\quad}$

f) $\times \underline{\quad} \left(\begin{array}{c} 3 : 8 \end{array} \right) \times 2$
   $\underline{\quad} : \underline{\quad}$

3. Fill in the blanks.

a) $\times \underline{\quad}$
   $4 : 3 = 12 : \underline{\quad}$
   $\times \underline{\quad}$

b) $\times \underline{\quad}$
   $8 : 7 = \underline{\quad} : 21$
   $\times \underline{\quad}$

c) $\times 5$
   $3 : 4 = \underline{\quad} : \underline{\quad}$
   $\times \underline{\quad}$

4. Multiply the first term by the same number the second term was multiplied by.

a) $3 : 4 = \underline{\quad\quad} : 16$

b) $6 : 7 = \underline{\quad\quad} : 35$

c) $2 : 5 = \underline{\quad\quad} : 20$

d) $4 : 5 = \underline{\quad\quad} : 20$

e) $1 : 5 = \underline{\quad\quad} : 25$

f) $2 : 3 = \underline{\quad\quad} : 18$

A **ratio table** has equivalent ratios in every row. To make a ratio table, make a list of equivalent ratios.

Example: 3 : 5 = 6 : 10 = 9 : 15 = 12 : 20

Then put each ratio into a separate row.

First Term	Second Term
3	5
6	10
9	15
12	20

5. a) Repeatedly draw 2 circles and 3 squares until you have 20 shapes.

b) Make a list of equivalent ratios using your picture.

2 : ___3___ = 4 : _____ = 6 : _____ = 8 : _____

c) Finish the ratio table.

Circles	Squares
2	3
4	
6	
8	

6. Use multiplication to complete a ratio table for each ratio.

a) 4 : 1

4	1
8	2
12	3
16	4

First row
First row × 2
First row × 3
First row × 4

b) 2 : 3

2	3

c) 5 : 2

5	2

7. Find the missing number in each ratio table.

a)

4	10
8	

b)

3	20
9	

c)

7	4
21	

d)

2	6
	24

8. Circle the tables that are ratio tables.

2	5
4	10

3	8
12	2

2	5
4	7

6	8
12	16

3	5
6	15

4	9
12	27

2	9
6	18

7	5
14	10

Two quantities are **proportional** if the T-table comparing their values is a ratio table.

9. Is the price of a drink proportional to its size?

a)

Apple Juice	
Cost ($)	Drink Size (oz)
1	4
2	8
3	16

_____

b)

Orange Juice	
Cost ($)	Drink Size (oz)
1	3
2	6
3	12

c)

Fruit Punch	
Cost ($)	Drink Size (oz)
2	8
4	16
6	24

_____

d)

Milk	
Cost ($)	Drink Size (mL)
2	100
4	300
6	500

_____

10. Are the children's allowances proportional to their ages?

a)

Family A	
Allowance ($)	Age (years)
8	5
16	10
24	15

_____

b)

Family B	
Allowance (¢)	Age (years)
25	4
100	8
200	12

c)

Family C	
Allowance ($)	Age (years)
8	3
16	6
24	12

_____

d)

Family D	
Allowance (¢)	Age (years)
5	2
15	6
30	12

_____

11. Did you need to look at the units ($ or ¢) to answer Questions 9 and 10? Explain.

_____

_____

8. Unit Ratios

In a **unit ratio**, one quantity is equal to 1. Unit ratios are easy to work with because 1 is easy to multiply and divide by.

Example: Each apple costs 30¢, so the unit ratio of cents to apples is 30 : 1.

1. Multiply to find the missing information.

   a) 1 book costs $5

      4 books cost __$20__

   b) 3 miles in 1 hour

      _____ miles in 5 hours

   c) 1 melon costs $3

      6 melons cost _____

2. Divide to find the missing information.

   a) 3 notebooks cost $24

      1 notebook costs _____

   b) 2 jackets cost $20.

      1 jacket costs _____

   c) 5 pears cost $20

      1 pear costs _____

3. Complete the ratio tables.

   a)
3	12
1	
5	

   ÷3   ×5

   b)
3	15
1	
8	

   ÷   ×

   c)
4	12
1	
5	

4. Which is a better deal?

   a) 3 T-shirts for $24   or   5 T-shirts for $45

      1 T-shirt for _____   1 T-shirt for _____

   b) 5 pens for 35¢   or   4 pens for 32¢

      1 pen for _____   1 pen for _____

   c) 7 CDs for $56   or   6 CDs for $42

      1 CD for _____   1 CD for _____

   d) 8 DVDs for $72   or   6 DVDs for $48

      1 DVD for _____   1 DVD for _____

Bonus ▶ Which is the best deal? Hint: Which price is better than 1 T-shirt for $10?

   8 T-shirts for $92   28 T-shirts for $273   35 T-shirts for $357

5. The unit ratio for 3,506 : 14,024 is 1 : 4. What is the unit ratio for 14,024 : 3,506? _____

In a ratio table, all the rows are equivalent ratios. So each row is equivalent to the same unit ratio.

6. Find the unit ratio in each row. Then circle the tables that are ratio tables.

a)

8	40	*1 : 5*
10	50	*1 : 5*
11	55	*1 : 5*

b)

5	15	____
6	18	____
9	27	____

c)

2	8	____
6	24	____
9	54	____

d)

6	42	____
10	70	____
11	66	____

e)

3	24	____
7	63	____
9	72	____

f)

4	24	____
9	54	____
10	60	____

7. Find the unit ratio. How can you get the second column from the first column?

a)

2	6
4	12
5	15

____1__ : __3____

____*multiply by 3*____

b)

4	16
3	12
8	32

____ : ____

_____

c)

7	35
8	40
100	500

____ : ____

_____

The **constant of proportionality** of a ratio is the number the unit ratio tells you to multiply by.

Example: The unit ratio for the ratio 5 : 20 is 1 : 4. The constant of proportionality is 4.

8. Find the constant of proportionality. Then find the missing number in the ratio table.

a)

2	6
3	*9*

3

b)

5	15
	18

____

c)

4	20
6	

____

d)

2	
3	12

____

e)

	16
20	80

____

f)

4	
9	45

____

9. Tape Diagrams and Ratio Problems

A **tape diagram** uses blocks of the same size to show a situation.

Example: There are 3 times as many girls as boys.

girls: [| |]
boys: [ ]

1. Use a tape diagram to represent the numbers of girls and boys.

   a) There are 4 times as many boys as girls.

   girls: [ ]
   boys: [| | |]

   b) There are twice as many girls as boys.

   girls:
   boys:

   c) There are 5 times as many boys as girls.

   girls:
   boys:

   d) There are 6 times as many girls as boys.

   girls:
   boys:

2. All the blocks are the same size. What is the size of one block?

   a) [2 | 2 | 2 | 2 | 2]
      [2 | 2] 6

   b)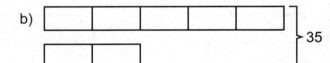
      } 35

   c) [| | |]
      [|] 20

   d)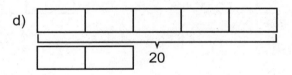
      20

3. Show the amount on the picture that represents 12 beads. What is the size of each block?

   a) There are 12 red beads.

   green: [2]
   red: [2 | 2 | 2 | 2 | 2 | 2]
            12

   b) There are 12 beads in total.

   green: [ ]
   red: [| |]

   c) There are 12 more red beads than green.

   green: [| |]
   red: [| | | |]

   d) There are 12 green beads.

   green: [| |]
   red: [|]

4. The bars below represent the number of red (r) and green (g) beads in a box. Fill in the blanks.

a) g:

r:

10 more red than green

1 block = _____ beads,

so _____ beads in total

b) g:

r:

35 beads altogether

1 block = _____, so _____ green beads

so _____ green beads

5. This tape diagram shows the number of girls and boys in a class. Each box represents the same number of students.

girls:

boys:

Complete the table.

If each box represents …	… then there are ___ girls	… and ___ boys
1 student	3	2
2 students	6	
3 students		
4 students		
5 students		

Is this a ratio table? _____

6. Use the model to find the number of red and green beads in each problem.

a) green beads : red beads = 2 : 3

10 more red beads than green beads

g:

r:

green: _____

red: _____

b) green beads : red beads = 7 : 3

30 beads altogether

g:

r:

green: _____

red: _____

7. Find the number of cups of blue (b) and yellow (y) paint needed to make green paint.

a) blue paint : yellow paint = 4 : 5

45 cups altogether

b: ▢▢▢▢

y: ▢▢▢▢▢

blue: _____

yellow: _____

b) blue paint : yellow paint = 5 : 3

8 more cups of blue paint than yellow

b: ▢▢▢▢▢

y: ▢▢▢

blue: _____

yellow: _____

c) blue paint : yellow paint = 3 : 7

12 more cups of yellow paint than blue

b: ▢▢▢

y: ▢▢▢▢▢▢▢

blue: _____

yellow: _____

d) blue paint : yellow paint = 7 : 5

36 cups altogether

b: ▢▢▢▢▢▢▢

y: ▢▢▢▢▢

blue: _____

yellow: _____

e) blue paint : yellow paint = 4 : 7

33 more cups of yellow than blue

b:

y:

blue: _____

yellow: _____

f) blue paint : yellow paint = 5 : 2

42 cups of paint altogether

b:

y:

blue: _____

yellow: _____

8. Draw a model to answer the question.

a) There are 35 students in a class. The ratio of girls to boys is 3 : 2. How many girls and how many boys are in the class?

b) There are 44 marbles in a jar. The marbles are blue and red. The ratio of blue marbles to red marbles is 5 : 6. How many red marbles and how many blue marbles are in the jar?

c) Clara collects American and Canadian stamps. She has 6 more American stamps than Canadian stamps. The ratio of Canadian to American stamps is 3 : 5. How many of each kind of stamp does she have?

9. Peter is 6 times as old as Ella.

a) What is the ratio of Peter's age to Ella's age?

b) Peter is 15 years older than Ella. How old are Peter and Ella?

10. Solving Proportions

1. There are 3 cats for every 2 dogs. Write the quantity you know in the correct column.
Write a question mark for the quantity you don't know.

		Cats : Dogs
a)	There are 12 dogs. How many cats are there?	3 : 2 = ___ : ___
b)	There are 12 cats. How many dogs are there?	3 : 2 = ___ : ___
c)	There are 18 dogs. How many cats are there?	3 : 2 = ___ : ___
d)	There are 48 cats. How many dogs are there?	3 : 2 = ___ : ___

A **proportion** is an equation that shows two equivalent ratios. Example: 1 : 4 = 2 : 8

When a proportion is missing a number, finding the missing number is called **solving the proportion**.

Example: To solve the proportion 10 : 3 = 50 : ?, notice that $10 \times 5 = 50$, so the missing number
is $3 \times 5 = 15$.

---

2. Solve the proportions from Question 1 to fill in the blanks.

a) There are _____ cats.

b) There are _____ dogs.

c) There are _____ cats.

d) There are _____ dogs.

3. Five bus tickets cost $9. Write and solve a proportion to answer these questions.

a) How many bus tickets can you buy with $45?

dollars : bus tickets

= ___ : ___

= ___ : ___

b) How much will 45 bus tickets cost?

dollars : bus tickets

= ___ : ___

= ___ : ___

4. Jake can run 3 laps in 5 minutes. At the same rate …

a) how many laps can he run in 30 minutes?

laps : minutes

= ___ : ___

= ___ : ___

b) how long would 30 laps take?

laps : minutes

= ___ : ___

= ___ : ___

5. Solve the proportions. Did you multiply the rows or the columns?

a) Nina can run 4 laps in 10 minutes. At the same rate, how long will it take her to run 20 laps?

It will take _____ minutes to run 20 laps.

I multiplied the _____.

Laps	Minutes
4	10
20	?

b) A muffin recipe calls for 3 cups of flour for 12 large muffins. Tony has 5 cups of flour. How many muffins can he make?

He can make _____ muffins.

I multiplied the _____.

Cups of Flour	Muffins
3	12
5	?

c) Two centimeters on a map represents five actual kilometers. If a lake is 6 cm long on the map, what is its actual size?

The lake is _____ km long.

I multiplied the _____.

Map Size (cm)	Actual Size (km)

6. Two centimeters on a map represents eight actual kilometers. If a lake is 5 cm long on the map, what is its actual size?

7. A baseball field 360 ft long has first base and home plate 90 ft apart. Kim wants to make a baseball field with the same proportions in a park 120 ft long. How far from home plate should she put first base?

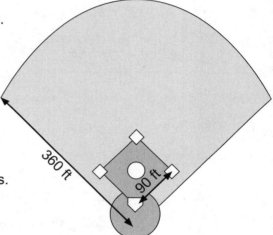

8. On a test with 30 math questions, Carl got 25 correct answers. At that rate, how many questions would he get right on a test with 90 questions?

9. An animal shelter has 4 dogs for every 5 cats. The shelter estimates that it spends $25 per month on each cat, and $40 per month on each dog. The shelter has a total of 45 cats and dogs. How much does it spend each month on all of the animals?

10. Zara wants to make 40 cups of orange paint. She uses 3 cups of red paint for every 5 cups of yellow paint. She already has 12 cups of red paint, but no yellow paint.

a) How much red paint does she need to buy?

b) How much yellow paint does she need to buy?

c) Paint costs $8 for each cup. How much does Zara need to spend on paint?

11. Integers

An **integer** is any one of these numbers: ..., −4, −3, −2, −1, 0, 1, 2, 3, 4, ...

1. Label the following integers on the number line with their letters.

T. 6   **O.** −3   **S.** −7   **P.** −5   **R.** 3

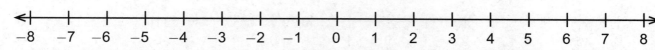

One integer is greater than another if it is:
- higher up on a vertical number line or
- farther right on a horizontal number line

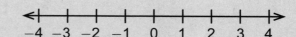

Write < for "is less than" and > for "is greater than."

2. a) Circle the integers on the number line: 2   −3   −7   −2   8

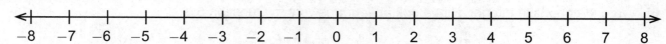

   b) Write the integers you circled in order from least to greatest.

   _____ < _____ < _____ < _____ < _____

3. Use the number line to answer the questions.

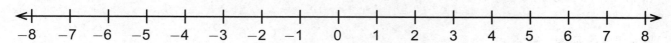

   a) Write < or > in the box.

   i) 2 ☐ 7   ii) −6 ☐ 5   iii) 8 ☐ −2   iv) −4 ☐ −6

   b) Put the integers into the boxes in order from greatest to least.

   4, −2, 7, −8, −1   ☐ > ☐ > ☐ > ☐ > ☐

   c) Write three integers that are less than −5. _____, _____, _____

   d) How many integers are between −4 and 2? _____

   e) Which integers are closer together, −3 and 3 or −4 and 4? _____

Integers that are **greater than 0** are called **positive integers**.
Integers that are **less than 0** are called **negative integers**.

4. How many negative integers are greater than (to the right of) −4? _____

5. Which other number is the same distance from 0 as the number marked?

a) 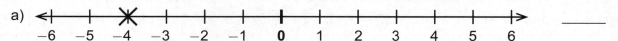 _____

b) _____

c) _____

d) _____

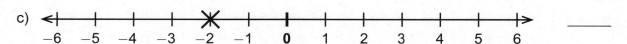

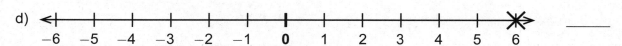

Opposite integers are the same distance from 0, but in opposite directions.

---

6. Write the opposite integer. Hint: Look at your answers to Question 5.

a) −4 _____   b) 3 _____   c) −2 _____   d) 6 _____

Positive numbers are sometimes written with a + in front.
Example: 3 can be written as 3 or +3, but −3 is written only as −3.

The opposite of an integer has the same whole number part, but the opposite sign (+ or −).
Example: The opposite of −100 is +100 or 100.

---

7. Write the opposite integer.

a) −83 _____   b) 76 _____   c) −800 _____   d) +510 _____

8. Use the number line to compare the positive numbers and their opposite negative numbers. Write < or > in each box.

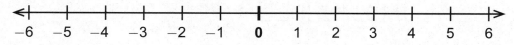

a) 2 ☐ 6 and −2 ☐ −6   b) 4 ☐ 1 and −4 ☐ −1

c) 5 ☐ 3 and −5 ☐ −3   d) 4 ☐ 6 and −4 ☐ −6

e) 3 ☐ 4 and −3 ☐ −4   f) 4 ☐ 0 and −4 ☐ −0

9. Make a prediction by writing < or > in the box.

835 < 846, so −835 ☐ −846.

10. Read the numbers from left to right. Circle the first pair of different digits you find.
Then write the greater number in the box.

a) 8 2, 4 ⑥ 3
    8 2, 4 ⑤ 8

b) ③ 8 4, 6 0 7
        3, 8 4 6

c) 8 5, 6 4 1
    9 5, 3 8 0

11. Write the correct inequality sign ($<$ or $>$) in the box.

a) 8,653 ☐ 8,486

b) 15,332 ☐ 16,012

c) 9,000 ☐ 7,999

d) 2,382 ☐ 589

e) 3,289 ☐ 10,104

f) 9,614 ☐ 90,614

> If you can compare positive numbers, you can compare their opposite negative numbers.
> Example: 30 is **less than** 40, so -30 is **greater than** -40.

12. Compare the positive integers, then compare the negative integers.

a) 5,438 ☐ 5,416

So $-5,438$ ☐ $-5,416$.

b) 35,463 ☐ 32,574

So $-35,463$ ☐ $-32,574$.

c) 90,608 ☐ 9,608

So $-90,608$ ☐ $-9,608$.

d) 72,035 ☐ 2,035

So $-72,035$ ☐ $-2,035$.

e) 863 ☐ 51,382

So -863 ☐ $-51,382$.

f) 85,417 ☐ 85,423

So $-85,417$ ☐ $-85,423$.

13. Do you need to compare the numbers 58 and 47 to compare -58 to $+47$? Explain. _____

_____

_____

14. Compare the fractions. Hint: Look at the signs first. Only look at the number parts
if you have to.

a) $-\dfrac{2}{5}$ ☐ $-\dfrac{4}{5}$

b) $-\dfrac{3}{4}$ ☐ $+\dfrac{1}{4}$

c) $-\dfrac{2}{3}$ ☐ $-\dfrac{1}{3}$

d) $-\dfrac{1}{2}$ ☐ $-\dfrac{3}{5}$

e) $+\dfrac{2}{3}$ ☐ $-\dfrac{3}{4}$

f) $-\dfrac{2}{3}$ ☐ $-\dfrac{3}{5}$

$= -\dfrac{}{10}$ $= -\dfrac{}{10}$

$= +\dfrac{}{12}$ $= -\dfrac{}{12}$

$= -\dfrac{}{15}$ $= -\dfrac{}{15}$

12. Integers in the Real World

Integers can be used to describe opposite directions from a chosen point. This point becomes the 0.

Examples:

- Temperature: degrees warmer than 0°F (+), or degrees colder than 0°F (−)
- Elevation: feet above sea level (+), or feet below sea level (−)
- Time zones: hours ahead of London, England (+), or hours behind London, England (−)

1. Write the integer to represent the situation. Include the units.

a) three degrees colder than 0°F ___−3°F___

b) four degrees warmer than 0°F _____

c) two feet above sea level ___+2 feet___

d) eight feet below sea level _____

e) five hours ahead of London, England _____

f) four hours behind London, England _____

g) thirty-four meters below sea level _____

h) eight hundred seven degrees warmer than 0°F _____

+45°F is warmer than +32°F, so the integer +42 is greater than +32.

2. The thermometer shows average temperatures of the eight planets in our solar system.

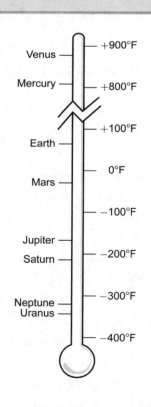

a) Which planet is warmest? _____

Its temperature is about _____ °F.

b) Which planet is coldest? _____

Its temperature is about _____ °F.

c) How many planets are warmer than Earth? _____

d) How many planets are colder than Earth? _____

e) About what is Earth's average temperature? _____

f) Which planet is about 300°F colder than Earth?

_____

g) About how much warmer is Mercury than Earth? _____ °F

Integers can be used to describe opposite values that cancel each other out.

Examples:

- Money: gaining money (+) and losing the same amount of money (−)
- Football: gaining yards (+) and losing the same number of yards (−)
- +/− rating: points in favor (+) and the same number of points against (−)

3. Write the integer that represents the situation. Include the units.

a) a gain of $5 _____

b) a loss of $9 _____

c) 4 points against _____

d) 3 points for _____

e) a gain of 2 yards in football _____

f) a loss of 3 yards in football _____

4. Show the gains and losses by marking the letters on the number line.

A. a gain of $4   **B.** a loss of $3   **C.** a gain of $5   **D.** a loss of $6

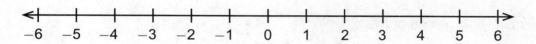

A bank statement shows a **credit** (+) when you add money to your account, and a **debit** (−) when you take money out of your account.

5. Write the integer that represents the action. Include the units.

a) a debit of $3   b) a credit of $5   c) a debit of $4   d) a credit of $7

___−$3___   _____   _____   _____

6. Four people have bank account balances.

Jake +$3   **Sally** +$6   **Ethan** −$4   **Mandy** −$5

a) Show each person's balance on the number line.

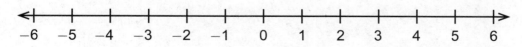

b) Write the four names in order from least balance to greatest balance.

_____ < _____ < _____ < _____

c) Whose bank account balance would you most like to have? _____

d) Whose bank account balance would you least like to have? _____

13. Adding Gains and Losses

1. Was it a good day (+) or a bad day (−)?

   a) + 5 − 3 __+__   b) + 3 − 5 _____   c) − 4 + 3 _____   d) + 6 − 9 _____

   e) − 3 + 2 _____   f) − 6 + 7 _____   g) + 7 − 2 _____   h) + 7 − 10 _____

2. How much was gained or lost overall?

   a) + 6 − 5   b) − 5 + 3   c) + 5 − 5   d) − 6 + 6

   _____   _____   _____   _____

   e) + 4 + 2   f) − 1 − 3   g) + 6 − 2   h) + 3 − 3

   _____   _____   _____   _____

To add many gains and losses:

Step 1: Circle the gains.

Step 2: Add the gains and losses separately.

Example: (+ 3) − 4 − 5 (+ 6)(+ 2) − 5 (+ 1)
= + 12 − 14 = −2

---

3. Circle the gains. How much was gained or lost overall?

   a) (+ 3) − 2 − 8 (+ 4)   b) + 6 + 5 − 3 − 7 + 6 − 4

      = + 7 − 10

      = −3

   c) − 5 − 6 + 9 − 8 + 10   d) − 9 + 7 − 2 + 1 + 1

   e) − 1 − 1 − 1 − 1   f) + 1 − 2 + 3 − 4 + 5 − 6 + 7 − 8

   Bonus ▶ Find an easier way to add + 1 − 2 + 3 − 4 + 5 − 6 + 7 − 8.

4. Cancel out as much as you can before adding.

a) $\cancel{-3} + 5 \cancel{+3} - 8$
$= +5 - 8 = -3$

b) $+5 - 4 \cancel{-3} + 2 \cancel{+3}$
$= \boxed{+5} - 4 \boxed{+2}$
$= +7 - 4 = +3$

c) $+9 - 5 - 6 + 5 + 3 - 9$

d) $+1 + 2 + 3 - 2 - 3 - 4$

e) $-7 + 4 + 5 - 4 + 7 + 6 - 1$

f) $+3 + 2 - 8 + 7 - 3 - 5 + 8$

g) $-8 + 5 + 3 - 7 - 5 + 7 + 5$

h) $-6 + 4 + 8 - 5 - 4 - 8 - 1$

Pairs that add to 10 are easy to see. When a positive pair adds to $+10$ and a negative pair adds to -10, you can cancel them out.

Example: $+4 + 6 - 3 - 5 - 7 = -5$ because $+4 + 6$ and $-3 - 7$ cancel each other out.

---

5. Cancel out pairs that add to $+10$ with pairs that add to -10. Then add the integers.

a) $+5 - 4 + 5 - 3 - 7$

b) $+8 + 3 + 2 - 1 - 9$

c) $+6 + 2 - 5 + 4 - 7 - 2 - 3 - 5 + 10$

d) $-1 + 2 - 3 + 5 + 8 + 5 - 4 - 7 - 6$

Bonus ▶ Cancel out pairs that add to $+100$ with pairs that add to -100. Then add the integers.

a) $-50 + 40 - 30 - 20 + 60 - 80$

b) $+62 - 41 - 59 + 38 - 69$

14. Integers

> **Integers** include positive whole numbers, negative whole numbers, and zero.
>
> An integer is any of the numbers: ..., −4, −3, −2, −1, 0, +1, +2, +3, +4, ...
>
> You can represent integers on a number line. Positive numbers do not need to have the + sign
>
>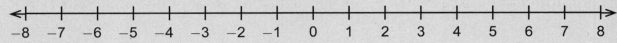

1. Label the integers on the number line with their letters.

   U. −5   **E.** 3   **R.** 4   **N.** −7   **M.** −2   **B.** −1   **S.** +6

   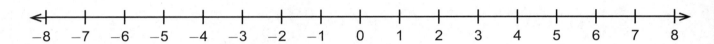

> A number line shows how the numbers compare.
>
> 2 is **greater** than −3; 2 is farther to the **right** on the number line.   We write 2 > −3.
>
> −5 is **less** than −1; −5 is farther to the **left** on the number line.   We write −5 < −1.

2. Circle the larger integer.

   a) ⑤, −3   b) −2, 4   c) −3, −7   d) −8, 0

3. a) Circle the integers −5, 3, −7, 4, 0, and −1 on the number line.

   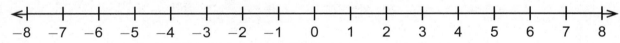

   b) Write the integers in order from least to greatest. _____ < _____ < _____ < _____ < _____ < _____

   c) Write the integers in order from greatest to least. _____ > _____ > _____ > _____ > _____ > _____

4. Write the integers −15, 23, 0, −8, −17, 14, and −1 from least to greatest.

   _____ < _____ < _____ < _____ < _____ < _____ < _____

> Integers are used in many everyday situations to describe numbers that are compared to zero.
>
> Examples: −30°C is 30 degrees below the temperature at which water freezes (0°C).
>
>   +30,000 ft is 30,000 ft above sea level (0 ft).

5. Write an integer for the situation.

   a) A gain in weight of 10 lb. _____   b) A decrease of $235 in a bank account. _____

   c) A golf score that is 3 strokes below par. _____   d) A gain in the stock market of 250 points. _____

You can use ⊕ to represent (+1) and ⊖ to represent (−1).

Examples: ⊕⊕⊕ represents (+3). ⊖⊖ represents (−2).

6. Draw a diagram to represent the integer.

   a) (−3)   b) (+2)   c) (−4)   d) (+5)

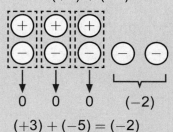

A gain of \$1 (+1) followed by a loss of \$1 (−1) is the same as no gain or loss. We write (+1) + (−1) = 0.

You can represent (+1) + (−1) with a diagram: ⊕⊖

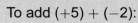

   To add (+3) + (−5):   To add (+5) + (−2):

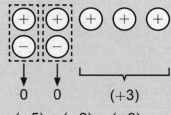

     0   0   0 (−2)   0   0   (+3)

    (+3) + (−5) = (−2)   (+5) + (−2) = (+3)

7. Use a diagram to add the integers.

   a) (+4) + (−2)   b) (+3) + (−7)   c) (+4) + (+2)   d) (−4) + (−2)

To add integers without a diagram, think of a contest between the positives and negatives. Who won the contest: the positives or the negatives? By how many did they win?

Question	Who Won?	By How Many?	Answer
(+3) + (−5)	negatives	2	(+3) + (−5) = (−2)
(+7) + (−4)	positives	3	(+7) + (−4) = (+3)
(−3) + (−2)	negatives	5	(−3) + (−2) = (−5)

8. Add without using a diagram.

   a) (+7) + (−2) =   b) (−8) + (+5) =   c) (−6) + (−3) =   d) (−5) + (−4) =

   e) (+5) + (+4) =   f) (−3) + (−6) =   g) (−3) + (−3) =   h) (+6) + (−8) =

9. Add without using a diagram.

   a) (+5) + (−2) + (−4) =   b) (−3) + (−2) + (+6) =

   c) (+8) + (−3) + (+4) =   d) (−3) + (−5) + (+6) =

   e) (−1) + (−4) + (−3) =   f) (+3) + (−5) + (+2) =

To show how we subtract integers, we remove the integers from the diagram. If necessary, we can add zeros in the form of ⊕ ⊖ so there will be enough positives or negatives to remove.

(+5) − (+2) = (+3)

(+3) − (−2) = (+5)

Add 2 groups of zero so we can take away 2 negatives

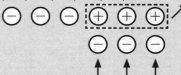

(−3) − (+3) = (−6)

Add 3 groups of zero so we can take away 3 positives

10. Use a diagram to subtract the integers.

a) (+4) − (+5) b) (−2) − (+3) c) (−3) − (−2) d) (−3) − (−4)

Opposite integers are the same distance from 0, but on opposite sides of 0 on the number line.

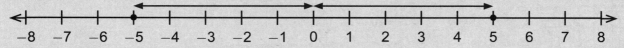

Example: −5 and 5 are both 5 units from 0. They are opposite integers.

11. Find the opposite integer.

a) (−3) _____ b) (+4) _____ c) (+8) _____ d) (−12) _____

Subtracting an integer is the same as adding its opposite integer.

(+3) − (−2) = (+3) + (+2)

Adding 2 zeros in the form of (+1) + (−1) twice and then taking away the 2 negatives is the same as adding (+2).

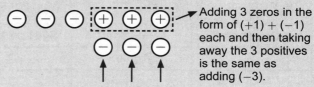

(−3) − (+3) = (−3) + (−3)

Adding 3 zeros in the form of (+1) + (−1) each and then taking away the 3 positives is the same as adding (−3).

12. Subtract by adding the opposite integer.

a) (+3) − (−4) b) (−4) − (+2) c) (+7) − (−3) d) (−3) − (−5)

= (+3) + (+4) = (−4) + (−2)

= (+7) = (−6)

e) (+2) − (+8) f) (−6) − (−2) g) (−1) − (+5) h) (−4) − (−7)

13. After the bank accidentally charged Rachel $5 in service fees, her account balance was $45. The bank corrected the mistake and returned the money to Rachel's account. Use integer subtraction to show that her balance is now $50.

15. Factors

There are only three ways to write 4 as a product of two whole numbers:

$1 \times 4 = 4$ $2 \times 2 = 4$ $4 \times 1 = 4$

The numbers that appear in the products are called the **factors** of 4.
The factors of 4 are the numbers 1, 2, and 4.

1. Write the whole number that makes the equation true. If no whole number makes the equation true, write ✕ in the box.

   a) $3 \times \boxed{4} = 12$ b) $4 \times \boxed{\times} = 18$ c) $2 \times \boxed{} = 20$ d) $3 \times \boxed{} = 14$

2. Write "yes" or "no." Use your answers to Question 1 to explain your answer.

   a) Is 3 a factor of 12? _Yes_ because _4 makes the equation true_ .

   b) Is 4 a factor of 18? _No_ because _no number makes the equation true_ .

   c) Is 2 a factor of 20? _____ because _____ .

   d) Is 3 a factor of 14? _____ because _____ .

---

2 and 3 are a **factor pair** of 6 because $2 \times 3 = 6$.

---

3. List the factor pairs of each number. List each pair only once.

   a) 6   b) 8   c) 9

   __1__ and __6__   _____ and _____   _____ and _____

   __2__ and __3__   _____ and _____   _____ and _____

4. Alice lists the factor pairs of 12 by using a chart. When a number is not a factor, she writes an ✕ in the second column.

   a) Why didn't Alice list 13 as a first factor?

   _____

   b) Use Alice's chart to write the factors of 12.

   _____ , _____ , _____ , _____ , _____ , _____

   c) Use Alice's chart to write the factor pairs of 12.

   _____ and _____

   _____ and _____

   _____ and _____

First Factor	Second Factor
1	12
2	6
3	4
4	3
5	✕
6	2
7	✕
8	✕
9	✕
10	✕
11	✕
12	1

5. Use Alice's method to find all the factor pairs of each number.

a) 14   b) 15   c) 16   d) 18   e) 20   f) 24   g) 25

6. Use the top half of each chart to finish the bottom half.

a) 18

First Factor	Second Factor
1	18
2	9
3	6
6	3
	2
	1

b) 30

First Factor	Second Factor
1	30
2	15
3	10
5	6
	5
	3
	2
	1

c) 36

First Factor	Second Factor
1	36
2	18
3	12
4	9
6	6

To list all the factors of a given number, stop when you get a number that is already part of a factor pair.

7. Make a chart to find all the factor pairs. There might be more rows in the chart than you need.

a) 20

First Factor	Second Factor
1	20
2	10
4	5
5	STOP

b) 81

First Factor	Second Factor
1	81
3	27
9	9
STOP	

c) 32

First Factor	Second Factor

d) 35

First Factor	Second Factor

e) 44

First Factor	Second Factor

f) 56

First Factor	Second Factor

JUMP Math Accumula

> The **greatest common factor (GCF)** of two numbers is the greatest number that is a factor of both numbers.

8. a) Find and list all the factors of each number. You can make a chart if it helps.

   i) 36   ii) 42   iii) 99

   _____   _____   _____

   _____   _____   _____

   b) Use your answers from part a) to find the greatest common factor of …

   i) 36 and 42 _____   ii) 36 and 99 _____   iii) 42 and 99 _____

9. Make an equivalent fraction by dividing the numerator and denominator by the same number.

   a) $\dfrac{2 \div 2}{10 \div 2} = \dfrac{1}{5}$ b) $\dfrac{12 \div 3}{18 \div 3} =$ c) $\dfrac{812 \div 2}{826 \div 2} =$

> Making an equivalent fraction with smaller numbers is called **reducing the fraction**.
> A fraction is in **lowest terms** if it cannot be reduced further.
>
> When a fraction is in lowest terms, the GCF of its numerator and denominator is 1.
>
> Example: $\dfrac{6}{8}$ in lowest terms is $\dfrac{3}{4}$. The GCF of 3 and 4 is 1.

10. Find the GCF of the numerator and denominator. Is the fraction in lowest terms?

Fraction	$\dfrac{8}{10}$	$\dfrac{3}{8}$	$\dfrac{6}{9}$	$\dfrac{6}{5}$	$\dfrac{7}{8}$	$\dfrac{7}{4}$	$\dfrac{10}{8}$	$\dfrac{12}{9}$	$\dfrac{13}{8}$
GCF									
Lowest Terms									

11. Divide the numerator and denominator by their GCF.

   a) $\dfrac{6 \div 2}{10 \div 2} = \dfrac{3}{5}$ b) $\dfrac{8}{12}$ c) $\dfrac{5}{10}$

   d) $\dfrac{12}{16}$ e) $\dfrac{9}{12}$ f) $\dfrac{16}{18}$

   g) $\dfrac{25}{15}$ h) $\dfrac{70}{80}$ i) $\dfrac{85}{95}$

12. Are your answers to Question 11 in lowest terms? If not, find your mistake.

16. Adding and Subtracting Fractions with the Same Denominator

1. Imagine moving the shaded pieces from each pie onto the empty pie plate. Show how much of the empty pie plate would be filled, then write a fraction for the amount.

a)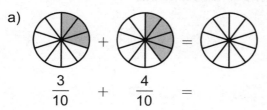

$$\frac{3}{10} \quad + \quad \frac{4}{10} \quad =$$

b)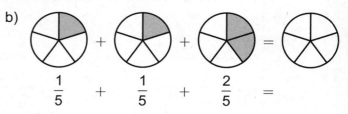

$$\frac{1}{5} \quad + \quad \frac{1}{5} \quad + \quad \frac{2}{5} \quad =$$

2. Subtract by taking away the second amount.

a) $\dfrac{5}{8} - \dfrac{2}{8} =$

$$\frac{1}{8} + \frac{1}{8} + \frac{1}{8} + \boxed{\frac{1}{8} + \frac{1}{8}}$$

b) $\dfrac{6}{7} - \dfrac{4}{7} =$

$$\frac{1}{7} + \frac{1}{7} + \frac{1}{7} + \frac{1}{7} + \frac{1}{7} + \frac{1}{7}$$

3. Add or subtract.

a) $\dfrac{3}{5} + \dfrac{1}{5} =$

b) $\dfrac{3}{8} + \dfrac{3}{8} + \dfrac{1}{8} =$

c) $\dfrac{6}{5} - \dfrac{3}{5} =$

d) $\dfrac{9}{100} - \dfrac{2}{100} =$

4. Start at zero. Move right to add a positive number. Move left to add a negative number.

a) $+ \dfrac{1}{5} + \dfrac{2}{5} = \boxed{}$

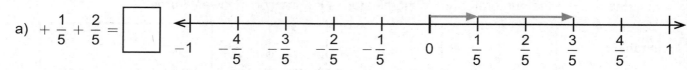

b) $+ \dfrac{1}{5} - \dfrac{4}{5} = \boxed{}$

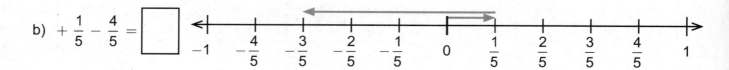

c) $- \dfrac{2}{5} + \dfrac{3}{5} = \boxed{}$

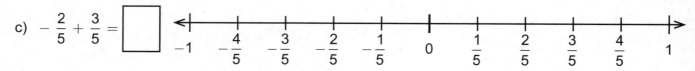

d) $- \dfrac{2}{5} - \dfrac{3}{5} = \boxed{}$

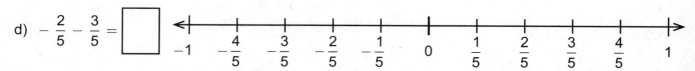

$+\dfrac{5}{9} - \dfrac{1}{9}$ and $-\dfrac{5}{9} + \dfrac{1}{9}$ are opposite numbers because each number being added is opposite.

$+\dfrac{5}{9} - \dfrac{1}{9} = \dfrac{4}{9}$, so $-\dfrac{5}{9} + \dfrac{1}{9} = -\dfrac{4}{9}$

5. Evaluate by using opposites.

a) $+\dfrac{7}{5} - \dfrac{3}{5} = \boxed{}$

$-\dfrac{7}{5} + \dfrac{3}{5} = \boxed{}$

b) $+\dfrac{6}{4} + \dfrac{1}{4} = \boxed{}$

$-\dfrac{6}{4} - \dfrac{1}{4} = \boxed{}$

c) $+\dfrac{3}{1,000} + \dfrac{4}{1,000} = \boxed{}$

$-\dfrac{3}{1,000} - \dfrac{4}{1,000} = \boxed{}$

$+1 - 4 = -3$ so $+1$ fifth -4 fifths $= -3$ fifths

$$+\dfrac{1}{5} \quad - \quad \dfrac{4}{5} \quad = \quad -\dfrac{3}{5}$$

6. Write the addition without brackets. Then evaluate.

a) $\left(+\dfrac{3}{8}\right) + \left(-\dfrac{5}{8}\right) = +\dfrac{3}{8} - \dfrac{5}{8} = -\dfrac{2}{8}$

b) $\left(-\dfrac{4}{3}\right) + \left(-\dfrac{4}{3}\right) =$

c) $\left(+\dfrac{2}{7}\right) + \left(+\dfrac{4}{7}\right) =$

d) $\left(-\dfrac{5}{7}\right) + \left(+\dfrac{1}{7}\right) =$

e) $\left(+\dfrac{2}{5}\right) + \left(-\dfrac{6}{5}\right) =$

f) $\left(-\dfrac{3}{8}\right) + \left(-\dfrac{2}{8}\right) =$

g) $\left(-\dfrac{2}{9}\right) + \left(+\dfrac{5}{9}\right) =$

Bonus ▶ $\left(+\dfrac{4}{8}\right) + \left(-\dfrac{5}{8}\right) + \left(+\dfrac{1}{8}\right) =$

7. Subtract by adding the opposite number of what you are subtracting.

a) $\left(-\dfrac{7}{8}\right) - \left(-\dfrac{1}{8}\right) = \left(-\dfrac{7}{8}\right) + \left(+\dfrac{1}{8}\right)$

$= -\dfrac{7}{8} + \dfrac{1}{8}$

$= -\dfrac{6}{8}$

b) $\left(-\dfrac{1}{8}\right) - \left(+\dfrac{2}{8}\right) =$

c) $\left(+\dfrac{6}{4}\right) - \left(-\dfrac{3}{4}\right)$

d) $\left(-\dfrac{4}{9}\right) - \left(+\dfrac{7}{9}\right)$

e) $\left(-\dfrac{2}{5}\right) - \left(-\dfrac{7}{5}\right)$

f) $\left(+\dfrac{5}{11}\right) - \left(+\dfrac{7}{11}\right)$

17. Mixed Numbers and Improper Fractions

A **mixed number** is a mixture of a whole number and a fraction. An **improper fraction** has a numerator larger than the denominator.

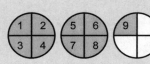

1. Write these fractions as mixed numbers and as improper fractions

   a)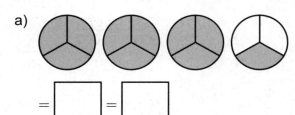

      = ☐ = ☐

   b)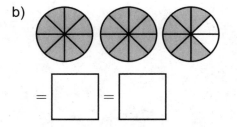

      = ☐ = ☐

2. Shade the amount of pie given by the mixed number. Then write an improper fraction.

   a) $3\frac{1}{2}$  ____

   b) $2\frac{3}{4}$ 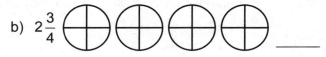 ____

   c) $2\frac{2}{3}$  ____

   d) $3\frac{2}{5}$ 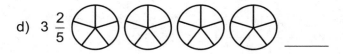 ____

3. Shade the area given by the improper fraction. Then write a mixed number.

   a) $\frac{7}{3}$ 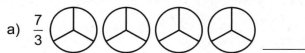 ____

   b) $\frac{17}{6}$ 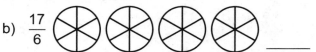 ____

   c) $\frac{13}{5}$ ____

   d) $\frac{21}{8}$ ____

4. Draw a picture to find out which is greater.

   a) $3\frac{1}{2}$ or $\frac{5}{3}$
   b) $1\frac{4}{5}$ or $\frac{11}{5}$
   c) $\frac{15}{8}$ or $\frac{7}{3}$
   d) $\frac{13}{4}$ or $2\frac{2}{3}$

5. Do you need to compare $\frac{1}{4}$ and $\frac{2}{9}$ to compare $6\frac{1}{4}$ and $5\frac{2}{9}$? Explain.

How many quarter pieces are in $2\frac{3}{4}$ pies?

There are 4 quarter pieces in 1 pie.

So there are 11 quarter pieces altogether.

There are 2 × 4 quarters in 2 pies.

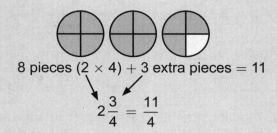

8 pieces (2 × 4) + 3 extra pieces = 11

$2\frac{3}{4} = \frac{11}{4}$

6. Find the number of **halves** in each amount.

a) 1 pie = _____ halves

b) 2 pies = _____ halves

c) 3 pies = _____ halves

d) $3\frac{1}{2}$ pies = _____ halves

e) $4\frac{1}{2}$ pies = _____ halves

f) $5\frac{1}{2}$ pies = _____ halves

7. Each pie has 3 pieces, so each piece is a third. Find the number of **thirds** in each amount.

a) 1 pie = ___*3 thirds*_____

b) 2 pies = _____

c) 5 pies = _____

d) $5\frac{1}{3}$ pies = _____

e) $2\frac{2}{3}$ pies = _____

f) $4\frac{2}{3}$ pies = _____

8. A box holds 4 cans, so each can is a fourth. Find the number of cans each amount holds.

a) 2 boxes hold _____ cans.

b) $2\frac{1}{4}$ boxes hold _____ cans.

9. Write the mixed number as an improper fraction.

a) $1\frac{4}{6} = \frac{\quad}{6}$

b) $5\frac{1}{2} = \frac{\quad}{2}$

c) $2\frac{3}{5} = \frac{\quad}{\quad}$

d) $3\frac{2}{8} = \frac{\quad}{\quad}$

e) $3\frac{1}{5} = \frac{\quad}{\quad}$

f) $2\frac{6}{8} = \frac{\quad}{\quad}$

g) $3\frac{6}{10} = \frac{\quad}{\quad}$

h) $6\frac{3}{10} = \frac{\quad}{\quad}$

10. Look at your answers to Question 9. When the fraction part of the mixed number is in lowest terms, is the improper fraction also in lowest terms? _____

11. These pies are each cut into four pieces. There are 15 pieces of pie in total. How many whole pies are there and how many pieces are left over?

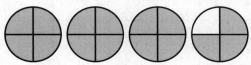

15 ÷ 4 = _____ R _____

How many whole pies are in $\dfrac{13}{4}$ pies?

There are 13 pieces altogether, and each pie has 4 pieces: **13 ÷ 4 = 3 Remainder 1**

There are 3 whole pies and 1 quarter left over: 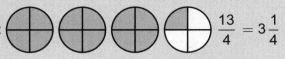 $\dfrac{13}{4} = 3\dfrac{1}{4}$

12. Find the number of whole pies in each amount by dividing.

a) $\dfrac{6}{2}$ pies = _____ whole pies   b) $\dfrac{12}{3}$ pies = _____ whole pies   c) $\dfrac{24}{4}$ pies = _____ whole pies

13. Find the number of whole pies and the number of pieces remaining by dividing.

a) $\dfrac{5}{2}$ pies = ___2___ whole pies and ___1___ half pie = $2\dfrac{1}{2}$ *pies*

b) $\dfrac{11}{2}$ pies = _____ whole pies and _____ half pie =

c) $\dfrac{7}{3}$ pies   d) $\dfrac{19}{4}$ pies   e) $\dfrac{17}{5}$ pies   f) $\dfrac{15}{8}$ pies   **Bonus ▶** $\dfrac{70}{9}$ pies

14. Divide the numerator by the denominator to write each improper fraction as a mixed number.

a) $\dfrac{16}{3}$ 16 ÷ 3 = ___5___ R ___1___   b) $\dfrac{19}{6}$ 19 ÷ 6 = _____ R _____   c) $\dfrac{18}{4}$ 18 ÷ 4 = _____ R _____

so $\dfrac{16}{3} = 5\dfrac{1}{3}$ so $\dfrac{19}{6} =$ so $\dfrac{18}{4} =$

d) $\dfrac{3}{2}$ e) $\dfrac{5}{4}$ f) $\dfrac{8}{3}$ g) $\dfrac{15}{4}$ h) $\dfrac{22}{5}$ i) $\dfrac{32}{5}$

15. Write a mixed number and an improper fraction for the total number of liters.

1 L

16. Write a mixed number and an improper fraction for the length of the rope.

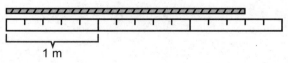

1 m

Since $\dfrac{7}{4} = 1\dfrac{3}{4}$, their opposites are equal too: $-\dfrac{7}{4} = -1\dfrac{3}{4}$.

17. Complete the chart.

Mixed Number	$-2\dfrac{3}{4}$	$-3\dfrac{2}{5}$		$-4\dfrac{1}{2}$				$-1\dfrac{3}{8}$
Improper Fraction	$-\dfrac{11}{4}$		$-\dfrac{7}{5}$		$-\dfrac{8}{3}$	$-\dfrac{9}{4}$	$-\dfrac{11}{3}$	

JUMP Math Accumula

18. Adding and Subtracting Mixed Numbers

$1\frac{3}{8}$ $\qquad$ $2\frac{4}{8}$ $\qquad$ $1 + 2 = 3$ and $\frac{3}{8} + \frac{4}{8} = \frac{7}{8}$, so $1\frac{3}{8} + 2\frac{4}{8} = 3\frac{7}{8}$.

1. Add by adding the parts and the wholes separately.

a) $2\frac{1}{5} + 4\frac{3}{5} =$ $\qquad$ b) $7\frac{1}{4} + 1\frac{2}{4} =$ $\qquad$ c) $2\frac{1}{5} + 4\frac{3}{5} =$

d) $6\frac{2}{8} + 3\frac{5}{8} =$ $\qquad$ e) $4\frac{3}{7} + 5\frac{2}{7} =$ $\qquad$ f) $3\frac{1}{9} + 7\frac{4}{9} =$

You can add mixed numbers by changing them both to improper fractions.

$1 \times 5 + 3 \qquad 2 \times 5 + 4$

Example: $1\frac{3}{5} + 2\frac{4}{5} \quad = \quad \frac{8}{5} + \frac{14}{5}$

$\qquad = \quad \frac{22}{5}$

$\qquad = \quad 4\frac{2}{5}$ because $22 \div 5 = 4$ R 2

Write your answer as a mixed number because the numbers you are adding are given in that form.

---

2. Write the mixed number as an improper fraction.

a) $5\frac{1}{8} = \frac{41}{8}$ $\quad$ b) $4\frac{1}{8} =$ $\quad$ c) $1\frac{3}{8} =$ $\quad$ d) $3\frac{5}{8} =$ $\quad$ e) $2\frac{7}{8} =$ $\quad$ f) $6\frac{4}{8} =$

3. Use your answers to Question 2 to add the mixed numbers. Write your answer as a mixed number.

a) $5\frac{1}{8} + 4\frac{1}{8} =$ $\qquad$ b) $1\frac{3}{8} + 3\frac{5}{8} =$ $\qquad$ c) $2\frac{7}{8} + 6\frac{4}{8} =$

d) $1\frac{3}{8} + 2\frac{7}{8}$ $\qquad$ e) $6\frac{4}{8} + 4\frac{1}{8}$ $\qquad$ f) $1\frac{3}{8} + 6\frac{4}{8}$

4. a) Raj adds $1\frac{3}{5} + 2\frac{4}{5}$ and gets $3\frac{7}{5}$, but $\frac{7}{5} > 1$, so he writes $3\frac{7}{5} = 3 + \frac{7}{5} = 3 + 1\frac{2}{5} = 4\frac{2}{5}$.

Is the answer correct?

b) Use Raj's method to add $2\frac{5}{9} + 1\frac{8}{9}$. Check by adding another way.

5. Add using Raj's method. You will need to change the improper fraction to a whole number.

$$1\frac{3}{5} + 2\frac{3}{5} + 3\frac{4}{5} =$$

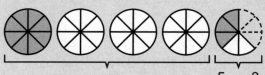

To subtract $4\frac{5}{8} - 1\frac{3}{8}$, subtract the wholes and parts separately.

$$4 - 1 = 3 \qquad \frac{5}{8} - \frac{3}{8} = \frac{2}{8} \qquad \text{So } 4\frac{5}{8} - 1\frac{3}{8} = 3\frac{2}{8}.$$

6. Subtract the wholes and parts separately.

a) $7\frac{3}{5} - 4\frac{1}{5} =$

b) $5\frac{2}{4} - 2\frac{1}{4} =$

c) $8\frac{7}{9} - 4\frac{2}{9} =$

7. Write the mixed numbers or whole numbers as improper fractions, then subtract. Write your answer as a mixed number or whole number.

a) $6\frac{1}{3} - 2\frac{2}{3} = \frac{19}{3} - \frac{8}{3}$

$$= \frac{11}{3}$$

$$= 3\frac{2}{3}$$

b) $3\frac{2}{5} - 1\frac{4}{5} =$

c) $5\frac{7}{10} - 2\frac{7}{10} =$

8. Look at your answer to Question 7.c). How could you have predicted the answer?

_____

_____

9. Subtract $9\frac{1}{4} - 5\frac{3}{4}$ by writing $9\frac{1}{4}$ as $8 + 1\frac{1}{4} = 8 + \frac{5}{4}$. Then check your answer by subtracting another way.

10. Add the positive and negative numbers by first changing them to improper fractions

a) $+3\frac{4}{6} - 2\frac{5}{6}$

b) $-8 + 3\frac{5}{7}$

c) $-7\frac{5}{8} - 3\frac{6}{8}$

11. Subtract by first changing the mixed numbers to improper fractions.

a) $-2\frac{7}{8} - \left(-5\frac{3}{8}\right) = -2\frac{7}{8} + 5\frac{3}{8}$

$$= -\frac{23}{8} + \frac{43}{8}$$

$$= +\frac{20}{8} = 2\frac{4}{8} = 2\frac{1}{2}$$

b) $+2\frac{5}{9} - \left(-3\frac{4}{9}\right) =$

c) $-6\frac{1}{8} - \left(+2\frac{5}{8}\right)$

d) $+3\frac{4}{7} - \left(+5\frac{6}{7}\right)$

e) $-6\frac{1}{8} - \left(-4\frac{4}{8}\right)$

Bonus ▶ $-3\frac{2}{8} - 4\frac{5}{8} - 2\frac{5}{8} - 1\frac{7}{8}$

12. Subtract $\left(-2\frac{3}{4}\right) - \left(-5\frac{1}{4}\right)$ two ways.

a) Locate the numbers on the number line and use their distance apart.

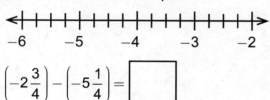

$$\left(-2\frac{3}{4}\right) - \left(-5\frac{1}{4}\right) = \boxed{}$$

b) Add the opposite number.

$$\left(-2\frac{3}{4}\right) - \left(-5\frac{1}{4}\right) = -2\frac{3}{4} + \boxed{}$$

c) Did you get the same answer both ways? If not, find your mistake.

13. A viperfish is $\frac{7}{8}$ miles below sea level, a depth of $-\frac{7}{8}$ miles. A fangtooth is $1\frac{7}{8}$ miles below the viperfish. At what depth is the fangtooth?

19. Adding and Subtracting Fractions with Different Denominators

You can add or subtract fractions with different denominators.

Step 1: Find the lowest common multiple of the denominators.

Step 2: Create equivalent fractions with that denominator.

Example: $\frac{1}{3} + \frac{2}{5}$

The LCM of 3 and 5 is 15.

$\frac{1}{3} = \frac{5}{15}$ and $\frac{2}{5} = \frac{6}{15}$

So $\frac{1}{3} + \frac{2}{5}$ and $\frac{5}{15} + \frac{6}{15} = \frac{11}{15}$.

The **lowest common denominator** (**LCD**) of two fractions is the lowest common multiple (LCM) of the denominators.

1. Find the LCD of the pair of fractions. Then write what number you multiplied the numerator and denominator by.

   a) $\frac{2 \times 2}{2 \times 3} + \frac{1}{6}$

   LCD = __6__

   b) $\frac{1}{4} + \frac{5}{8}$

   LCD = _____

   c) $\frac{1}{6} + \frac{4}{9}$

   LCD = _____

2. Add or subtract the fractions by changing them to equivalent fractions. The denominators should be equal to the LCD of the fractions.

   a) $\frac{1}{5} + \frac{3}{4}$

   =

   =

   b) $\frac{5}{12} + \frac{2}{3}$

   =

   =

   c) $\frac{5}{6} - \frac{3}{10}$

   =

   =

3. Add or subtract. Write your answer in lowest terms.

   a) $\frac{3}{7} + \frac{1}{14}$

   b) $\frac{3}{5} - \frac{4}{15}$

   c) $\frac{15}{28} - \left(\frac{3}{4} - \frac{5}{7} \right)$

4. Do the first subtraction, then use opposites to do the second subtraction. Do your rough work in your notebook.

   a) $\frac{2}{5} - \frac{3}{10} = \boxed{}$

   $\frac{3}{10} - \frac{2}{5} = \boxed{}$

   b) $\frac{2}{3} - \frac{1}{4} = \boxed{}$

   $\frac{1}{4} - \frac{2}{3} = \boxed{}$

   c) $\frac{5}{8} + \frac{1}{4} = \boxed{}$

   $-\frac{5}{8} - \frac{1}{4} = \boxed{}$

same sign ———— To add two numbers ———— opposite sign

Add the absolute values. The sign is the same as for both numbers.

Subtract the absolute values. The sign is the same as for the number with the larger absolute value.

5. Add or subtract. Write your answer in lowest terms.

a) $-\dfrac{3}{4} - \dfrac{2}{8}$

$= -\dfrac{6}{8} - \dfrac{2}{8}$

$= -\dfrac{8}{8} = -1$

b) $+\dfrac{1}{6} - \dfrac{1}{3}$

c) $-\dfrac{4}{5} - \dfrac{2}{3}$

d) $-\dfrac{5}{8} + \dfrac{2}{8}$

e) $-2\dfrac{3}{4} - 3\dfrac{1}{6}$

f) $+4\dfrac{5}{6} + 2\dfrac{7}{10}$

g) $-\dfrac{2}{5} + \dfrac{1}{2}$

h) $-\dfrac{1}{6} - \dfrac{1}{2}$

i) $-5\dfrac{1}{6} + 2\dfrac{4}{9}$

j) $+1\dfrac{3}{5} + 1\dfrac{1}{4}$

k) $+3\dfrac{3}{8} - 1\dfrac{1}{8}$

l) $+2\dfrac{2}{5} - 1\dfrac{1}{8}$

6. Drop the brackets to subtract.

a) $-\dfrac{1}{8} - \left(+\dfrac{1}{4}\right)$

$= -\dfrac{1}{8} - \dfrac{1}{4}$

$= -\dfrac{1}{8} - \dfrac{2}{8}$

$= -\dfrac{3}{8}$

b) $-\dfrac{7}{8} - \left(-\dfrac{1}{8}\right)$

c) $+2\dfrac{2}{3} - \left(-3\dfrac{1}{4}\right)$

d) $-3\dfrac{5}{6} - \left(-2\dfrac{3}{8}\right)$

e) $-2\dfrac{1}{2} - \left(+2\dfrac{1}{3}\right)$

f) $+2\dfrac{3}{5} - \left(+3\dfrac{1}{8}\right)$

7. A dragonfish was found at a depth of $-1\dfrac{1}{4}$ miles. The deepest ever fish was found at a depth of $-4\dfrac{4}{5}$ miles. How much deeper is that?

20. Multiplying a Fraction and a Whole Number

1. The picture shows 15 dots divided into 5 equal groups. Fill in the blank.

   a) $\frac{1}{5}$ of 15 = _____　　b) $\frac{2}{5}$ of 15 = _____　　c) $\frac{3}{5}$ of 15 = _____　　d) $\frac{4}{5}$ of 15 = _____

2. Draw the correct number of dots in each group. Then circle the amount, and fill in the blank.

   a) $\frac{2}{3}$ of 15　

   so $\frac{2}{3}$ of 15 = _____

   b) $\frac{3}{4}$ of 12　◯ ◯ ◯ ◯

   so $\frac{3}{4}$ of 12 = _____

   c) $\frac{5}{6}$ of 24　◯ ◯ ◯ ◯ ◯ ◯

   so $\frac{5}{6}$ of 24 = _____

   d) $\frac{3}{8}$ of 24　◯ ◯ ◯ ◯ ◯ ◯ ◯ ◯

   so $\frac{3}{8}$ of 24 = _____

3. Draw a picture to find $\frac{3}{5}$ of 10.

   $\frac{3}{5}$ of 10 = _____

Andy finds $\frac{2}{3}$ of 12 as follows:

Step 1: He finds $\frac{1}{3}$ of 12 by dividing 12 by 3.　　**Step 2:** Then he multiplies the result by 2.

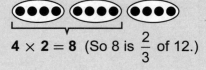

12 ÷ 3 = 4 (So 4 is $\frac{1}{3}$ of 12.)　　**4 × 2 = 8** (So 8 is $\frac{2}{3}$ of 12.)

---

4. Find the following amounts using Andy's method.

   a) $\frac{1}{3}$ of 6 = _____ so $\frac{2}{3}$ of 6 = _____　　b) $\frac{1}{4}$ of 8 = _____ so $\frac{3}{4}$ of 8 = _____

   c) $\frac{2}{3}$ of 15 = _____　　d) $\frac{3}{5}$ of 25 = _____

   e) $\frac{4}{5}$ of 20 = _____　　f) $\frac{5}{7}$ of 21 = _____

In mathematics, the word "of" can mean multiply.

"2 groups of 4" means 2×4

$2 \times 4 = 8$

"$\frac{1}{2}$ of a group of 6" means $\frac{1}{2} \times 6$

$\frac{1}{2} \times 6 = 3$

5. Calculate the product by calculating the fraction of the whole number.

a) $\frac{2}{3} \times 9 = \frac{2}{3}$ of $9 = \underline{\quad 6 \quad}$ ← $(2 \times 9) \div 3$

b) $\frac{1}{2} \times 10 = \frac{1}{2}$ of $10 = \underline{\quad\quad}$

c) $\frac{2}{5} \times 10$

d) $\frac{3}{4} \times 12$

e) $\frac{1}{3} \times 15$

f) $\frac{2}{3} \times 12$

6. How can you tell from your answers to Question 5 that $\frac{1}{2} > \frac{2}{5}$?

REMINDER: Multiplication by a whole number is a short form for repeated addition.

Example: $5 \times 7 = 7 + 7 + 7 + 7 + 7$

7. Imagine moving the shaded pieces from each pie onto the empty pie plate. Show how much of the empty pie plate would be filled. Then write a fraction for that amount.

a)

$\frac{3}{10} + \frac{3}{10} =$

b)

$\frac{1}{5} + \frac{1}{5} + \frac{1}{5} =$

c)

$5 \times$

$5 \times \frac{1}{6} =$

d)

$4 \times$

$4 \times \frac{2}{9} =$

$4 \times \frac{3}{5} = \frac{4 \times 3}{5} = \frac{12}{5}$

8. Multiply.

a) $10 \times \frac{4}{9} =$

b) $3 \times \frac{4}{5} =$

c) $7 \times \frac{7}{10} =$

d) $8 \times \frac{1}{3} =$

e) $8 \times \frac{3}{5} =$

f) $9 \times \frac{2}{5} =$

g) $5 \times \frac{4}{3} =$

h) $6 \times \frac{7}{2} =$

9. Multiply the same numbers, but in a different order.

$\dfrac{2}{3} \times 9 = \dfrac{2}{3}$ of $9 =$

$9 \times \dfrac{2}{3} =$

Did you get the same answer both times? If not, find your mistake.

10. Find the product. Write your answer in lowest terms.

a) $3 \times \dfrac{5}{6} = \dfrac{15}{6} = \dfrac{5}{2}$

b) $6 \times \dfrac{2}{3} = \dfrac{12}{3} = 4$

c) $4 \times \dfrac{3}{10} =$

d) $\dfrac{3}{4} \times 2 =$

e) $\dfrac{7}{6} \times 10 =$

f) $\dfrac{5}{8} \times 4 =$

You can multiply whole numbers by negative fractions, too!

$$3 \times (-4) = (-4) + (-4) + (-4)$$
$$= -4 - 4 - 4$$
$$= -12$$

$$3 \times \left(-\dfrac{1}{2}\right) = \left(-\dfrac{1}{2}\right) + \left(-\dfrac{1}{2}\right) + \left(-\dfrac{1}{2}\right)$$
$$= -\dfrac{1}{2} - \dfrac{1}{2} - \dfrac{1}{2}$$
$$= -\dfrac{3}{2}$$

---

11. Multiply by using repeated addition.

a) $5 \times (-3) = \underline{(-3) + (-3) + (-3) + (-3) + (-3)}$

$= \underline{\quad -3 - 3 - 3 - 3 - 3 \quad} = \underline{\quad}$

b) $4 \times (-2) = \underline{\hspace{6cm}}$

$= \underline{\hspace{5cm}} = \underline{\quad}$

c) $3 \times \left(-\dfrac{5}{8}\right) = \left(-\dfrac{5}{8}\right) + \left(-\dfrac{5}{8}\right) + \left(-\dfrac{5}{8}\right)$

$= \underline{\hspace{4cm}} = \underline{\quad}$

d) $2 \times \left(-\dfrac{3}{5}\right) = \underline{\hspace{5cm}}$

$= \underline{\hspace{4cm}} = \underline{\quad}$

12. Multiply.

a) $4 \times 5 = 20$

so $4 \times (-5) =$

b) $5 \times 3 = 15$

so $5 \times (-3) =$

c) $6 \times 4 = 24$

so $(-6) \times 4 =$

d) $\left(-\dfrac{2}{5}\right) \times 3 =$

e) $\left(-\dfrac{4}{3}\right) \times 5 =$

f) $10 \times \left(-\dfrac{3}{5}\right) =$

13. Grace gets 1 point for every correct answer on a test, and $-\dfrac{3}{4}$ points for every incorrect answer. She got 15 correct answers and 5 incorrect answers. How many points did she get in total?

21. Problems and Puzzles

1. Eddy is playing football. Add Eddy's team's gains and losses from its turn, then subtract the other team's gains and losses from its turn. How did Eddy's team do overall?

Eddy's Team	Other Team	Integer Subtraction	Eddy's Team's Overall Result
gains 7 yards	gains 3 yards	$+7 - (+3) = +4$	*gains 4 yards*
loses 7 yards	gains 3 yards		
gains 7 yards	loses 3 yards		
loses 7 yards	loses 3 yards		

2. At the South Pole, the average daily high temperature is $-26°C$ in January and $-56°C$ in July. How much warmer is the South Pole in January than in July?

3. Use pictures to show that $-2 + 1 = -2 - (-1)$.

$-2 = \ominus \ominus$ $-2 + 1 =$ $-2 - (-1) =$

4. Kate spins the spinner twice and adds the two results.

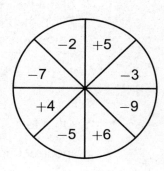

   a) What is the highest total she could score? _____

   b) What is the lowest total she could score? _____

   c) What is the largest possible difference between the two scores?

   _____

   d) How could she score zero? _____

5. a) Find $2 \times \frac{4}{5}$ and $3 \times \frac{4}{5}$. Show your answer on the number line.

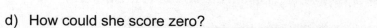

   b) Use $2 \times \frac{4}{5}$ and $3 \times \frac{4}{5}$ to predict $2\frac{1}{2} \times \frac{4}{5}$. _____

   Show your answer on the number line in part a).

Answer all problems in your notebook.

6. Jane lives in time zone +5 (that is, 5 hours ahead of London time). Bob is in time zone −4 (that is, 4 hours behind London time). How many hours ahead of Bob is Jane?

7. Mount Lamlam on the island of Guam is one of the tallest mountains in the world. Its peak is 406 m above sea level. It extends to 10,911 m below sea level. How tall is Mount Lamlam?

8. Do you expect the answer to $3\frac{1}{2} - 5\frac{3}{5}$ to be more than or less than −2? Explain your prediction, and then check it by doing the subtraction.

9. Find two fractions with different denominators and different signs (+ or −) that add to $\frac{11}{12}$.

10. Jin wants to center a picture on a wall. The picture is $3\frac{1}{3}$ feet wide. The wall is $10\frac{1}{2}$ feet wide. How far from each edge of the wall should he place the picture? Fill in the dimensions on the diagram to help you.

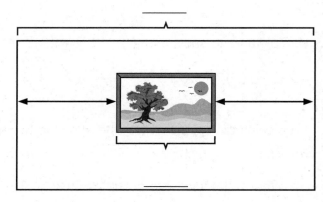

11. On a test, Tasha gets 1 point for each correct answer, $-\frac{1}{4}$ points for every incorrect answer, and $-\frac{1}{2}$ points for every question left blank. Tasha answered 12 questions correctly, 5 questions incorrectly, and left 3 questions blank.

    How many points did she get altogether?

12. a) Group the fractions that have the same denominators. Then add or subtract.

    i) $\frac{3}{4} + \frac{2}{5} - \frac{1}{4}$

    ii) $-\frac{7}{2} + \frac{3}{5} + \frac{3}{2}$

    iii) $-2\frac{3}{4} + 3\frac{1}{8} - 1\frac{1}{4}$

    b) Do part ii) of Question 12.a) without grouping the fractions first. Was it more work? Explain why or why not.

22. The Standard Method for Multiplication

How to solve $3 \times 42 = 3 \times 40 + 3 \times 2$

$$= 3 \times 4 \text{ tens} + 3 \times 2 \text{ ones}$$

Step 1

Multiply the ones digit by 3
(3×2 ones $= 6$ ones).

	4	2
×		3
		6

↑ ones

Step 2

Multiply the tens digit by 3
(3×4 tens $= 12$ tens).

Regroup 10 tens as 1 hundred.

	4	2
×		3
1	2	6

↑ hundreds   ↑ tens

---

1. Use **Steps 1** and **2** to find the product.

a)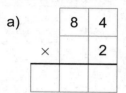

b)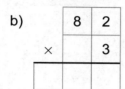

c)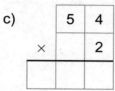

d)

e)
	7	2
×		3

How to solve $7 \times 53 = 7 \times 50 + 7 \times 3$

$$= 7 \times 5 \text{ tens} + 7 \times 3 \text{ ones}$$

Step 1

Multiply 3 ones by 7
($7 \times 3 = 21$).

	2	
	5	3
×		7
		1

Step 2

Regroup 20 ones as 2 tens.

---

2. Complete **Steps 1** and **2** of the multiplication.

a)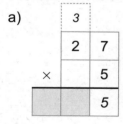

b)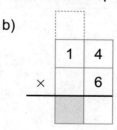

c)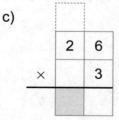

d)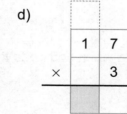

e)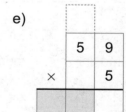

f)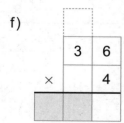

g)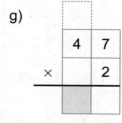

h)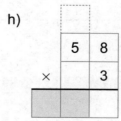

i)
	4	7
×		6

j)
	9	7
×		8

Step 3

Multiply 5 tens by 7
(7×5 tens $= 35$ tens).

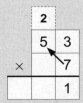

Step 4

Add 2 tens to the result
($35 + 2 = 37$ tens).

3. Complete **Steps 3** and **4** of the multiplication.

a)
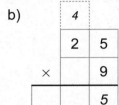

b)

c)

d)

e)
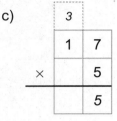
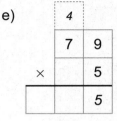

4. Complete **all steps** of the multiplication.

a) b) c) d) e)

5. Multiply by regrouping ones as tens.

a)
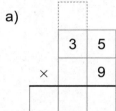

b)
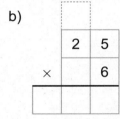

c)
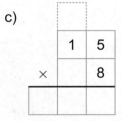

d)
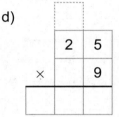

e)
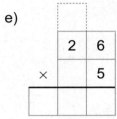

6. Multiply by regrouping when you need to.

a) b)
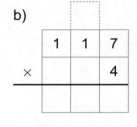

c)
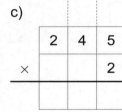

d)
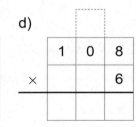

e)
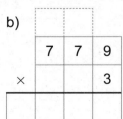
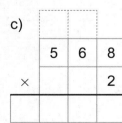

7. A dog is 16 years old. Multiply that by 7 to estimate the dog's age in dog years.

8. Anna has borrowed a library book for 21 days. She reads 8 pages each day. If the book is 165 pages long, will she need to renew the book?

JUMP Math Accumula

To multiply 37 × 20, first multiply 37 × 2, then multiply by 10.

This is how to record your answer on a grid:

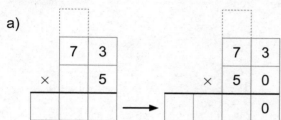

$\xrightarrow{\times 10}$

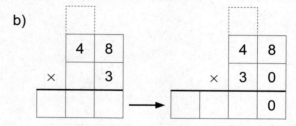

9. Multiply.

a)

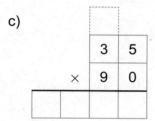

→

b)

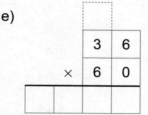

→

c)

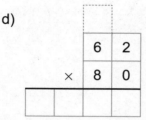

d)

e)

f)

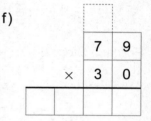

To multiply 37 × 25, split 25 into two numbers that are easier to multiply by. The picture shows why this works.

a multiple of 10 ↘   a 1-digit number ↙

$37 \times 25 = 37 \times \mathbf{20} + 37 \times \mathbf{5}$

$= 740 + 185$

$= 925$

$37 \times 25 \Bigl\{$

37×20
37×5

10. Multiply. Do your rough work in your notebook.

a) 11 × 57

11 × 50 = _____

11 × 7 = _____

so 11 × 57 = _____

b) 76 × 43

76 × 40 = _____

76 × 3 = _____

so 76 × 43 = _____

c) 95 × 16

95 × 10 = _____

95 × 6 = _____

so 95 × 16 = _____

d) 58 × 35

58 × 30 = _____

58 × 5 = _____

so 58 × 35 = _____

11. Multiply.

a) 58 × 70

b) 71 × 62

c) 84 × 23

d) 94 × 57

12. Is your answer to Question 11.a) double your answer to Question 10.d)? If not, find your mistake.

You can record the steps in multiplying 2-digit numbers on a grid.

Example: Find 37 × 25.

Step 1: Calculate 37 × 5.

Step 2: Calculate 37 × 20.

Step 3: Add the results.

	1	3	
	3	7	
×	2	5	
1	8	5	← 37 × 5
7	4	0	← 37 × 20
9	2	5	

13. Practice Step 1.

a)

	1	
2	4
×	1	3
	7	2	= 24 × 3

b)

	5	3
×	3	9

c)

	5	2
×	3	4

d)

	1	6
×	7	5

14. Practice Step 2.

a) *1*

	3	4
×	7	3
1	0	2	= 34 × 70

b) *1*

	6	9
×	6	2
1	3	8

c) *1*

	5	2
×	4	6
3	1	2

d) *3*

	6	7
×	3	5
3	3	5

15. Practice Steps 1 and 2.

Regrouping 35 × 20 →   ← Regrouping for 35 × 6

a)

	3	5
×	2	6
			= 35 × 6
		0	= 35 × 20

b)

	4	2
×	5	3

c)

	6	5
×	3	3

d)

	5	6
×	4	1

16. Multiply.

a)

	4	7
×	2	4
+			0

b)

	7	9
×	5	4
+			0

c)

	9	4
×	5	5

d)

	8	4
×	3	6

JUMP Math Accumula

23. Variables and Expressions

1. There are 5 people in one family. Write an addition expression for the number of chairs needed if the family has …

   a) 2 guests   b) 3 guests   c) 7 guests   d) n guests

   __5 + 2__   _____   _____   _____

> A **variable** is a letter or symbol that represents a number.

2. Evaluate the expression when $n = 5$.

   a) $n + 2 = 5 + 2$ b) $8 - n = 8 - 5$ c) $6 + n =$ d) $n - 4 =$

   $\quad = 7$ $\qquad = $ $\qquad =$ $\qquad =$

3. Evaluate the expression when n is the given value.

   a) $n + 3, \quad n = 7$ b) $n - 5, \quad n = 2$ c) $8 + n, \quad n = -3$ d) $-7 - n, \quad n = -2$

   $7 + 3 = 10$ $2 - 5 =$

4. The nth row of a theater has $n + 4$ seats. How many seats are in the 21st row? _____

5. The nth person in line waited for $10 + n$ minutes. How long did the 50th person wait in line? _____

6. It costs $3 to rent skates for an hour. Write a multiplication expression for the cost of renting skates for …

   a) 2 hours _____   b) 5 hours _____   c) 6 hours _____   d) n hours _____

7. Write an expression for the distance a car would travel at the given speed for the given amount of time.

   a) 60 miles per hour for 2 hours

   _____

   b) 80 miles per hour for 3 hours

   _____

   c) 50 miles per hour for h hours

   _____

   d) m miles per hour for 4 hours

   _____

> In a product of a number and a variable, the multiplication sign is usually dropped.
>
> Examples: $3 \times T$ can be written as $3T$ and $5 \times z$ can be written as $5z$.

8. Write the expression without multiplication signs.

   a) $8 \times r =$ __8r__   b) $2 \times s =$ _____   c) $4 \times P =$ _____   **Bonus ▶** $r \times s =$ _____

9. Write the expression with multiplication signs.

Bonus ▶

a) $3w =$ _ $3 \times w$ _   b) $5r =$ _____   c) $6W =$ _____ $8rT =$ _____

10. Renting skis cost $5 an hour. Write two expressions for the cost of renting skis for ...

a) h hours: _ $5 \times h$ _ or _ $5h$ _   b) t hours: _____ or _____

c) x hours: _____ or _____   d) n hours: _____ or _____

To evaluate $3h$ at $h = 5$, use brackets: $3h = 3(5)$—not 35!

11. Evaluate the expression for $n = 2$.

a) $5n = 5(2)$ b) $7n = 7(2)$ c) $11n$ d) $30{,}000n$

    $= 10$

12. Evaluate the expression at the given value of n.

a) $3n$, $n = 7$ b) $10n$, $n = 14$ c) $8n$, $n = 100$ d) $500n$, $n = 6{,}000$

13. The nth figure uses $5n$ squares. How many squares does the 10th figure use? _____

14. Renting a boat for n hours costs $6n$. How much does renting the boat for 4 hours cost? _____

15. Draw a rectangle when x is the given value.

	$2x$ x ☐	$x + 2$ x ☐
a) $x = 1$ cm		
b) $x = 2$ cm		
c) $x = 3$ cm		

24. Expressions with Two Operations

1. Evaluate the expression for $n = 4$.

   a) $3n + 5$

   $= 3(4) + 5$

   $= 12 + 5$

   $= 17$

   b) $15 - 2n$

   c) $9 + 4n$

   d) $3n - 20$

   e) $8 - 7n$

   f) $-3 + 2n$

2. Evaluate the expression for $x = -1$.

   a) $2x + 6$

   b) $3x + 4$

   c) $9x - 4$

   d) $2x - 5$

   e) $3 - 7x$

   f) $-5 - 2x$

3. Evaluate the expression for the given number.

   a) $5h + 2$, $h = 3$

   b) $2n - 3$, $n = 6$

   c) $3 - 5t$, $t = -4$

   d) $3m + 2$, $m = -\dfrac{1}{2}$

   e) $5t - \dfrac{3}{4}$, $t = \dfrac{5}{8}$

   f) $\dfrac{7}{5} - 2t$, $t = -\dfrac{3}{4}$

   g) $\dfrac{3}{2}w + 5$, $w = 3$

   h) $\dfrac{5}{8}r - 7$, $r = 8$

   i) $-3 + \dfrac{2}{5}s$, $s = 7$

> A **flat fee** is a fixed charge that does not depend on how long you rent an item.
>
> Example: It costs a flat fee of $7 to rent a boat, plus $3 for each hour you use the boat.

4. Write an expression for the amount you would pay to rent a boat for …

   a) 2 hours

   Flat fee: $9

   Hourly rate: $5 per hour

   $2 \times 5 + 9$

   b) 3 hours

   Flat fee: $4

   Hourly rate: $6 per hour

   _____

   c) 7 hours

   Flat fee: $5

   Hourly rate: $4 per hour

   _____

   d) *h* hours

   Flat fee: $5

   Hourly rate: $4 per hour

   $4h + 5$

   e) *t* hours

   Flat fee: $8

   Hourly rate: $3 per hour

   _____

   f) *w* hours

   Flat fee: $6

   Hourly rate: $5 per hour

   _____

5. Match the fee (left) for renting a windsurfing board to the correct algebraic expression (right).

   A $15 flat fee and $7 for each hour $15h + 7$

   $15 for each hour, no flat fee $7h + 15$

   A $7 flat fee and $15 for each hour $15h$

6. Write an expression for the cost. Use *n* for the variable.

   a) Umbrellas are on sale for $2 each. _____

   b) A copy shop charges $0.79 for each copy. _____

   c) A bus company charges a $10 flat fee, plus $5 per passenger. _____

   d) A boat company charges a $20 flat fee, plus $7 per passenger. _____

7. A company charges a $6 flat fee to rent a pair of skis, plus $3 for each hour you use the skis.
   The total is given by the expression $3h + 6$. Find the cost of renting a pair of skis for …

   a) 4 hours

   $3(4) + 6$

   $= 12 + 6$

   $= 18$

   b) 2 hours

   c) 5 hours

8. Socks cost $2 per pair. The cost of *n* pairs is $2n. Kyle says that the cost of 6 pairs is
   $26 and the cost of 7 pairs is $27. Explain how the mistakes were made.

   _____

   _____

A triangle has a mass of *t* kg and a circle has a mass of 1 kg.

The mass of △/t △/t is 2*t* kg and the mass of ①①① is 3 kg.

9. Write the mass of the set.

a) △/t △/t △/t ①

_____3t + 1_____ kg

b) ① ①

_____ kg

c) △/t △/t ① ① ①

_____ kg

d) △/t ① ① ①

_____ kg

An **algebraic expression** is an expression with at least one variable. Two algebraic expressions are equivalent if they have the same value for every value of the variable.

10. a) Write the mass as an expression.

  i) ① ① △/t has a mass of _____ kg

  ii) △/t ① ① has a mass of _____ kg

  b) Will the two pictures always have the same mass for the same value of *t*? _____

  Are the expressions *t* + 2 and 2 + *t* equivalent? _____

  c) Evaluate the expressions *t* + 2 and 2 + *t* when ...

  i) *t* = 0 _____   ii) *t* = 1 _____   iii) *t* = 5 _____   **Bonus** ▶ *t* = −3 _____

  d) The expressions *t* + 2 and 2 + *t* are equivalent. Circle the property that shows this.

    the associative property   the commutative property

11. a) Draw a picture beside each expression, using circles and triangles to show the mass.

  1 + 2*t*   2*t* + 1

  b) Are 1 + 2*t* and 2*t* + 1 equivalent? _____ How do you know? _____

  _____

  c) Evaluate the expressions from part a) when ...

  i) *t* = 0 _____   ii) *t* = 1 _____   iii) *t* = 5 _____   **Bonus** ▶ *t* = −3 _____

12. a) Draw a picture to show the masses of 3(4*t*) and (3 × 4)*t*.

  b) Are the expressions equivalent? How do you know?

  c) Evaluate the expressions 3(4*t*) and (3 × 4)*t* when ...

  i) *t* = 0   ii) *t* = 1   iii) *t* = 5   **Bonus** ▶ *t* = −3

  d) The expressions 3(4*t*) and (3 × 4)*t* are equivalent. Does this show the associative property, the commutative property, or the distributive property?

25. Adding and Subtracting Expressions

Remember: 3×2 is short for $2 + 2 + 2$. Similarly, $3x$ is short for $x + x + x$.

1. Write the sum as a product of a number and a variable.

   a) $x + x + x + x = $ _____

   b) $y + y + y = $ _____

2. Write the product as a sum.

   a) $4w = $ _____

   b) $5r = $ _____

3. Add by writing how many x's there are altogether.

   a) $\quad\quad 3x \quad\quad + \quad 2x$
   $$= x + x + x + x + x = \underline{\quad 5x \quad}$$

   b) $\quad\quad 4x \quad\quad + \quad\quad 3x$
   $$= x + x + x + x + x + x + x = \underline{\quad\quad}$$

   c) $\quad\quad x \quad\quad + \quad 6x$
   $$= \underline{\hspace{4cm}} = \underline{\hspace{2cm}}$$

   d) $\quad\quad 2x \quad\quad + \quad 2x$
   $$= \underline{\hspace{4cm}} = \underline{\hspace{2cm}}$$

4. Write two equivalent expressions for $6x$.

   $6x = x + x + x + x + x + x$
   $$= \underline{\quad\quad} + \underline{\quad\quad}$$

   $6x = x + x + x + x + x + x$
   $$= \underline{\quad\quad} + \underline{\quad\quad}$$

By the distributive property ...	And for any number x ...
$2 \times 4 + 3 \times 4 = (2 + 3) \times 4$	$2x + 3x = (2 + 3)x$
$4 + 4 + 4 + 4 + 4 = 4 + 4 + 4 + 4 + 4$	$x + x + x + x + x = x + x + x + x + x$

5. Add by adding the numbers in front of the variable.

   a) $3x + 4x = (3 + 4)x = $ _____

   b) $8x + x = (8 + 1)x = $ _____

   c) $4x + 4x = ($ _____ $)x = $ _____

   d) $3x + 8x + 9x = ($ _____ $)x = $ _____

6. Evaluate both expressions. Are your answers the same? If not, find your mistake.

	$2x + 5x$	$7x$
a) $x = 3$	$2(3) + 5(3) = 6 + 15 = 21$	$7(3) = 21$
b) $x = 5$		
c) $x = \dfrac{3}{5}$		

$5x - 3x = 2x$ $x + x + \boxed{x + x + x}\nearrow$

7. Subtract by taking away x's.

a) $6x - 2x =$ _____

$x + x + x + x + \boxed{x + x}\nearrow$

b) $9x - 4x =$ _____

$x + x + x + x + x + x + x + x + x$

c) $7x - 5x =$ _____

$x + x + x + x + x + x + x$

d) $10x - 6x =$ _____

$x + x + x + x + x + x + x + x + x + x$

8. Draw x's and take some away to subtract.

a) $5x - 3x =$ _____

b) $8x - 5x =$ _____

9. Add and subtract. Hint: Circle the x's being added and evaluate those first.

a) $\boxed{7x} - 4x + \boxed{3x} + \boxed{2x} - x$

$= 12x - 5x = 7x$

b) $6x - x - x - x - x - x$

c) $-2x + 3x - 5x - x + 4x$

d) $7x - 2x + 4x - 8x - 2x + x$

REMINDER: $+(+) = +$ $+(-) = -$ $-(+) = -$ $-(-) = +$

10. Add and subtract.

a) $3x + (-2x) - (-6x) - (+4x) + (+7x) - (-3x)$

$= 3x - 2x + 6x - 4x + 7x + 3x$

$= 19x - 6x$

$= 13x$

b) $7x - (-2x) + (-3x) - (+5x) + (+4x)$

c) $-5x - (+3x) - (-2x) + (-7x) + (+4x) - (-8x)$

d) $-x + (-x) + (+x) - (-x) - (+x)$

26. Like Terms

Terms with the same variable are called **like** terms. Constant terms are also like terms.

To **simplify** expressions like the ones below, you can start by putting like terms together. Then add or subtract the like terms.

Examples: $7 + 8x + 2 + 5x = 8x + 5x + 7 + 2$
$$= 13x + 9$$

$7x + 2 - 5x + 3 = 7x - 5x + 2 + 3$
$$= 2x + 5$$

1. Simplify the expression. Start by putting like terms together.

a) $2x + 5 + 3x$

b) $3 + 4x + 7$

c) $8x + 5 + 3x + 2$

d) $3x + 4 + 7 + 6x$

e) $5x + 1 - 4 - 3x + 5$

f) $8x + 2 - 5x + 7 - 4 + x$

2. Find the perimeter (the distance around the shape). Then simplify the expression.

a)

$$\underline{ x + x + x + x = 4x }$$

b)

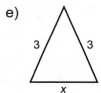

_____

c)

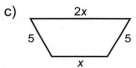

_____

d)

_____

e)

_____

f)

_____

3. Put like terms together to add the expressions.

a) $(10x + 3) + (5x - 4)$

$$= 10x + 3 + 5x - 4$$

$$= 10x + 5x + 3 - 4$$

$$= 15x - 1$$

b) $(3x + 7) + (5x - 3)$

c) $(7x + 6) + (-8x - 9)$

d) $(2x + 5) + (-3x + 1)$

$$7 - (2 + 1) = 7 - 2 - 1 \qquad\qquad 7 - (5 - 3) = 7 - 5 + 3$$
$$7 - (3 + 1) = 7 - 3 - 1 \qquad\qquad 7 - (6 - 3) = 7 - 6 + 3$$
$$7 - (4 + 1) = 7 - 4 - 1 \qquad\qquad 7 - (7 - 3) = 7 - 7 + 3$$

For any x, $\qquad\qquad\qquad\qquad$ For any x,

$$7 - (x + 1) = 7 - x - 1 \qquad\qquad 7 - (x - 3) = 7 - x + 3$$

4. Write the subtraction without brackets, then combine like terms to simplify.

a) $5 - (x + 1)$ $\qquad\qquad$ b) $8 - (x - 1)$ $\qquad\qquad$ c) $6 - (3x - 2)$

d) $7x - (x + 2)$ $\qquad\qquad$ e) $2x + 3 - (2x - 3)$ $\qquad\qquad$ f) $2x + 5 - (3x + 7)$

g) $3x + (5x - 4)$ $\qquad\qquad$ h) $3x - (5x - 4)$ $\qquad\qquad$ i) $(3x + 2) - (3x - 5)$

j) $(2 - 7x) + (3 - 5x)$ $\qquad\qquad$ k) $(2 - 7x) - (3 - 5x)$ $\qquad\qquad$ l) $(3x - 7) - (5 - 3x)$

5. Check your answer to Question 4 part e) for $x = 10$, $x = 11$, and one other value.

6. Ray hired Sun and Peter to help him move. Sun charged a $20 flat fee and $30 per hour. Peter charged $25 per hour.

a) Write an expression for Ray's total cost if Sun and Peter each work h hours.

_____

b) Write an expression for the difference in pay if Sun and Peter each work h hours.

_____

7. Tessa has nine children and hires two babysitters at a time. Tim charges $15 per hour with the first hour free, and Yu charges $10 per hour plus a flat fee of $20. Write an expression for Tessa's total cost, and say what the variable represents.

27. Coefficients and Constant Terms

An **equation** shows two expressions that are equal.

1. Circle the equations.

$5n - 3$ $n + 6 = 7$ $2 - x = 4$

$7 - 5x$ $9 = 8 + 3x + 4x$

$9 = 5 + 4$ $9 \times 3 + (8 - 4) \times 5$ $5(6x - 3)$

In an expression, the **coefficient** is the number of times that the variable is added.

Examples:

• $5x + 2 = x + x + x + x + x + 2$ has coefficient 5 because x is being added 5 times.

• $w - 7 = 1w - 7$ has coefficient 1 because w is being added once.

---

2. Write the coefficient.

a) $3a + 2$ _____

b) $m - 3$ _____

c) $3 + 8w$ _____

d) $2 + 6r$ _____

e) $9 + p$ _____

f) $s - 4$ _____

When the variable is subtracted, the coefficient is written as a negative number.

Examples:

• $3 - 4y$ has coefficient -4.

• $-5 - x$ has coefficient -1.

---

3. Write the coefficient.

a) $3 - m$ _____

b) $5 - 7w$ _____

c) $-6r - 3$ _____

In the expression $3a + 7b + 5$, the **coefficient of a** is 3 and the **coefficient of b** is 7.

---

4. Write the coefficient of x.

a) $3x + 4y + 7$ _____

b) $8x - y + 9$ _____

c) $2u + 4x - 5$ _____

d) $3u - 7x - 8$ _____

e) $9w + 3x + 8y$ _____

f) $-5 + 4w - 3x$ _____

5. The cost in dollars of s sandwiches and d drinks is $3s + 2d$.

a) Find the cost of 5 sandwiches and 4 drinks.

b) What does the coefficient of s tell you?

---

6. Evaluate the expression at the given values for the variables.

	$x = 1, y = 2$	$x = 2, y = 1$
a) $3x + y$	$3(1) + 2 = 3 + 2 = 5$	$3(2) + 1 = 6 + 1 = 7$
b) $5x - 2y$		
c) $2x - 3y$		

7. Simplify by combining like terms.

a) $2x + 3y + 4 + x + 5y + 7$

$= \underline{2x + x + 3y + 5y + 4 + 7}$

$= \underline{3x + 8y + 11}$

b) $7x - 5y + 2 - x + 2y + 6$

$= \underline{\hspace{4cm}}$

$= \underline{\hspace{4cm}}$

c) $-2x + 3 + 4y - 5x + 6y$

$= \underline{\hspace{4cm}}$

$= \underline{\hspace{4cm}}$

In an expression, the quantity without the variable is called the **constant term**.

Examples: • $3x + 4$ has constant term 4.
• $5x = 5x + 0$ has constant term 0.
• $7x - 5$ has constant term -5.

---

8. Write the constant term.

a) $3x + 4y + 7$ _____

b) $8x - y + 9$ _____

c) $2u + 4x - 5$ _____

d) $3u - 7x - 8$ _____

e) $9w + 3x + 8y$ _____

Bonus ▶ $8 - y - 3$ _____

9. What is -4, the coefficient or the constant term?

a) $4 - 4x$

b) $x - 4$

c) $-4 - x$

_____ _____ _____

10. It costs \$3 per hour to use the ski hill and \$10 to rent skis.

a) Write an expression for the cost of renting skis to go skiing for h hours. _____

b) In the expression, the coefficient is _____ and the constant term is _____ .

11. The cost of renting a bike for h hours is \$5h + 4$. Match each term to the correct item.

a) flat fee   5

   hourly rate   h

   hours rented   4

b) flat fee   constant term

   hourly rate   variable

   hours rented   coefficient

12. Evaluate the expression $7x - 4$ at $x = 0$. Is your answer the coefficient or the constant term?

28. Equivalent Expressions

> REMINDER: A triangle has a mass of *t* kg and a circle has a mass of 1 kg.
>
> The mass of △△ is 2*t* kg and the mass of ○○○ is 3 kg.

1. Write the mass of the set.

   a)    b) ○○○   c) △△△○   d) △○○○

   <u> 4*t* </u> kg   _____ kg   _____ kg   _____ kg

2. Draw triangles and circles to show each mass (given in kg).

   a) *t* + 2   ⟶   3(*t* + 2)   b) 2*t* + 1   ⟶   2(2*t* + 1)

      △△○

   c) 2*t* + 3   ⟶   3(2*t* + 3)   d) 3*t* + 1   ⟶   4(3*t* + 1)

3. Draw a picture for the expression. Write a new equivalent expression without brackets.

   a) 2(*t* + 4)   b) 2(3*t* + 2)   c) 3(2*t* + 1)   d) 3(4*t* + 1)

   <u> 2*t* + 8 </u>   _____   _____   _____

   e) 3(*t* + 2)   f) 2(5*t* + 1)   g) 4(3*t* + 4)   h) 5(2*t* + 1)

> REMINDER: By the associative property, $3(5w) = (3 \times 5)w = 15w$.

4. Multiply.

  a) $4(3r)$ b) $6(5s)$ c) $3(7w)$ d) $8(9x)$

  = _____   = _____   = _____   = _____

> By the distributive property, $3(2w + 5) = 3(2w) + 3(5)$
> $$= 6w + 15.$$

5. To multiply an expression by 4, multiply each term by 4.

  a) $4(x + 1)$ b) $4(x + 2)$ c) $4(2x + 1)$ d) $4(2x + 5)$

      $4x + 4$ _____   _____   _____

  e) $4(-x + 2)$ f) $4(3x - 2)$ g) $4(7 - 5x)$ h) $4(-3x - 4)$

  _____   _____   _____   _____

> You can simplify sums and differences of expressions.
> $7 - 2(3x + 4) = 7 - (6x + 8)$
> $$= 7 - 6x - 8$$
> $$= -1 - 6x$$

6. Simplify.

  a) $9x - 3(x + 4)$ b) $9x - (3x + 4)$ c) $9 - 3(2x + 4)$ d) $9 - 3(2x - 4)$

     $= 9x - (3x + 12)$

     $=$

  e) $7 - 2(3 - 8x)$ f) $8x - 3(4 - 5x)$ g) $2 - 4(3 - 2x)$ h) $4x - 3(-7 + 3x)$

  i) $(8x + 2) - 4(3 - 2x) + (3x - 5)$ j) $(5 + 4x) + (9 - 4x) - 3(-7 + 3x)$

  Bonus ▶ Write the expression without brackets, then simplify.

       $2(x + 2) + 3(x + 7) - 5(2x - 4)$

29. Decimal Fractions

> In a **decimal fraction**, the denominator is a power of ten.
>
> 10, 100, 1,000, 10,000, … are **powers of 10**.
>
> Example: $\dfrac{8}{100}$ is a decimal fraction.
>
> 5, 26, 111, 700, … are **not powers of 10**.
>
> Example: $\dfrac{8}{700}$ is not a decimal fraction.

1. Circle the decimal fractions.

$$\frac{3}{10} \qquad \frac{3}{21} \qquad \frac{53}{100} \qquad \frac{9}{26} \qquad \frac{7}{100} \qquad \frac{5}{35} \qquad \frac{63}{1,000} \qquad \frac{100}{15} \qquad \frac{125}{600} \qquad \frac{100}{52}$$

> Entire grid $= \dfrac{100}{100} = 1$ one
>
> 1 column $= \dfrac{10}{100} = \dfrac{1}{10} = 1$ tenth
>
> 1 square $= \dfrac{1}{100} = 1$ hundredth

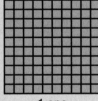
1 one

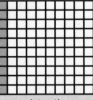
1 tenth

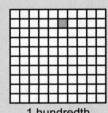
1 hundredth

2. Write two equivalent fractions for the shaded part of the grid.

a)

$$\frac{3}{10} = \frac{}{100}$$

b)

$$\frac{}{10} = \frac{}{100}$$

c)

$$\frac{}{10} = \frac{}{100}$$

3. Write an equivalent fraction with denominator 100.

a) $\dfrac{8 \times 10}{10 \times 10} = \dfrac{}{100}$

b) $\dfrac{3 \times 10}{10 \times 10} = \dfrac{}{100}$

c) $\dfrac{5}{10} = \dfrac{}{100}$

d) $\dfrac{4}{10} = \dfrac{}{}$

e) $\dfrac{9}{10} = \dfrac{}{}$

f) $\dfrac{6}{10} = \dfrac{}{}$

4. Write an equivalent fraction with denominator 1,000.

a) $\dfrac{9 \times 10}{100 \times 10} = \dfrac{}{1,000}$

b) $\dfrac{3}{100} = \dfrac{}{1,000}$

c) $\dfrac{4}{100} = \dfrac{}{1,000}$

d) $\dfrac{8 \times 100}{10 \times 100} = \dfrac{}{1,000}$

e) $\dfrac{3}{10} = \dfrac{}{1,000}$

f) $\dfrac{5}{10} = \dfrac{}{1,000}$

g) $\dfrac{6}{10} = \dfrac{}{}$

h) $\dfrac{6}{100} = \dfrac{}{}$

i) $\dfrac{1}{100} = \dfrac{}{}$

5. Write the equivalent hundredths and thousandths.

Tenths	$\frac{7}{10}$	$\frac{3}{10}$	$\frac{8}{10}$	$\frac{2}{10}$	$\frac{9}{10}$	$\frac{10}{10}$
Hundredths						
Thousandths						

Notice the pattern:

6. How many more zeros are in the second denominator? Add the same number of zeros to the numerator.

a) $\dfrac{9}{10} = \dfrac{}{100}$

b) $\dfrac{80}{100} = \dfrac{}{1,000}$

c) $\dfrac{4}{100} = \dfrac{}{1,000}$

d) $\dfrac{4}{10} = \dfrac{}{1,000}$

e) $\dfrac{6}{10} = \dfrac{}{1,000}$

f) $\dfrac{2}{10} = \dfrac{}{100}$

Bonus ▶ $\dfrac{30}{1,000} = \dfrac{}{10,000,000}$

7. Write the decimal fraction shown by the shaded part of the grid in four ways.

		$\dfrac{}{100}$	$\dfrac{}{10} + \dfrac{}{100}$	_____ hundredths	_____ tenths _____ hundredths
a)		$\dfrac{32}{100}$	$\dfrac{3}{10} + \dfrac{2}{100}$	_32_ hundredths	_3_ tenths _2_ hundredths
b)		$\dfrac{}{100}$	$\dfrac{}{10} + \dfrac{}{100}$	_____ hundredths	_____ tenths _____ hundredths
c)				_____ hundredths	_____ tenths _____ hundredths

COPYRIGHT © JUMP MATH: NOT TO BE COPIED. US EDITION

To add $\dfrac{9}{10} + \dfrac{4}{100} + \dfrac{8}{1{,}000}$, change all fractions to thousandths.

$$\dfrac{9 \times 100}{10 \times 100} + \dfrac{4 \times 10}{100 \times 10} + \dfrac{8}{1{,}000} = \dfrac{900}{1{,}000} + \dfrac{40}{1{,}000} + \dfrac{8}{1{,}000} = \dfrac{948}{1{,}000}$$

8. Add. Show your work.

a) $\dfrac{5 \times 100}{10 \times 100} + \dfrac{3 \times 10}{100 \times 10} + \dfrac{7}{1{,}000}$

$= \dfrac{500}{1{,}000} + \dfrac{30}{1{,}000} + \dfrac{7}{1{,}000} = \dfrac{537}{1{,}000}$

b) $\dfrac{2 \times 100}{10 \times 100} + \dfrac{8 \times 10}{100 \times 10} + \dfrac{6}{1{,}000}$

$= \dfrac{}{1{,}000} + \dfrac{}{1{,}000} + \dfrac{}{1{,}000} = \dfrac{}{1{,}000}$

c) $\dfrac{3 \times}{10 \times} + \dfrac{9 \times}{100 \times} + \dfrac{4}{1{,}000}$

$= \dfrac{}{1{,}000} + \dfrac{}{1{,}000} + \dfrac{}{1{,}000} = \dfrac{}{1{,}000}$

d) $\dfrac{3}{10} + \dfrac{3}{100} + \dfrac{3}{1{,}000}$

$= \dfrac{}{1{,}000} + \dfrac{}{1{,}000} + \dfrac{}{1{,}000} = \dfrac{}{1{,}000}$

9. Write the sum as a sum of fractions with the same denominator.

a) $\dfrac{1}{10} + \dfrac{6}{100} + \dfrac{2}{1{,}000} = \dfrac{100}{1{,}000} + \dfrac{60}{1{,}000} + \dfrac{2}{1{,}000} = \dfrac{162}{1{,}000}$

b) $\dfrac{6}{10} + \dfrac{7}{100} + \dfrac{5}{1{,}000} =$

c) $\dfrac{2}{10} + \dfrac{3}{100} + \dfrac{4}{1{,}000} =$

10. Add the tenths and hundredths.

a) $\dfrac{1}{10} + \dfrac{9}{100} = \underline{\qquad}$

b) $\dfrac{6}{10} + \dfrac{7}{100} = \underline{\qquad}$

c) $\dfrac{2}{10} + \dfrac{7}{100} = \underline{\qquad}$

d) $\dfrac{3}{10} + \dfrac{1}{100} = \underline{\qquad}$

11. Add.

a) $\dfrac{9}{10} + \dfrac{6}{100} + \dfrac{7}{1{,}000} =$

b) $\dfrac{8}{10} + \dfrac{8}{100} + \dfrac{8}{1{,}000} =$

c) $\dfrac{9}{10} + \dfrac{4}{1{,}000} =$

d) $\dfrac{7}{100} + \dfrac{9}{1{,}000} =$

e) $\dfrac{5}{100} + \dfrac{3}{1{,}000} =$

f) $\dfrac{4}{10} + \dfrac{4}{1{,}000} =$

30. Place Value and Decimals

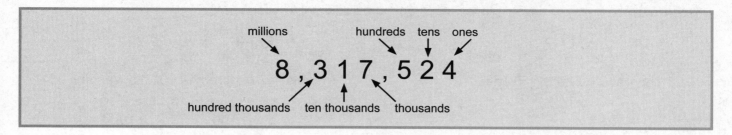

1. Write the place value of the underlined digit.

a) 56,2̲36 _____hundreds_____

b) 1̲,956,336 _____

c) 8,25̲6,601 _____

d) 7,103,25̲6 _____

e) 2,5̲89,143 _____

f) 3,921̲,052 _____

g) 903,74̲6 _____

h) 2,605,4̲16 _____

i) 3,459,0̲12 _____

j) 7,0̲18,762 _____

2. Write the place value of the digit 6 in each of the numbers below.
Hint: First underline the 6 in each number.

a) 36̲,589 _____thousands_____

b) 6,308,503 _____

c) 35,906 _____

d) 612 _____

e) 2,642 _____

f) 3,461,528 _____

g) 43,261 _____

h) 162,775 _____

i) 1,643,001 _____

j) 6,704,021 _____

k) 7,306 _____

l) 9,596,000 _____

3. Write the number in the place value chart.

	Millions	Hundred Thousands	Ten Thousands	Thousands	Hundreds	Tens	Ones
a) 8,413,712							
b) 83,406							
c) 7,503,219							
d) 2,499							
e) 23							
f) 775,206							
g) 8,003,005							

Decimals are a way to record place values based on decimal fractions.

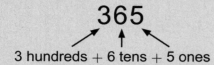

3 hundreds + 6 tens + 5 ones

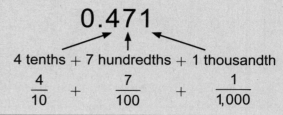

4 tenths + 7 hundredths + 1 thousandth

$$\frac{4}{10} + \frac{7}{100} + \frac{1}{1,000}$$

4. Write the decimal as the sum of a whole number and decimal fractions.

a) $2.17 = \underline{2} + \frac{1}{10} + \frac{7}{100}$

b) $3.24 = \underline{} + \frac{}{10} + \frac{}{100}$

c) $8.31 = \underline{} + \frac{}{10} + \frac{}{100}$

d) $5.02 = \underline{} + \frac{}{10} + \frac{}{100}$

e) $0.46 = \underline{} + \frac{}{10} + \frac{}{100}$

f) $9.15 = \underline{} + \frac{}{10} + \frac{}{100}$

g) $3.206 = \underline{} + \frac{}{10} + \frac{}{100} + \frac{}{1,000}$

h) $3.104 = \underline{} + \frac{}{10} + \frac{}{100} + \frac{}{1,000}$

i) $6.521 = \underline{} + \frac{}{10} + \frac{}{100} + \frac{}{1,000}$

j) $7.602 = \underline{} + \frac{}{10} + \frac{}{100} + \frac{}{1,000}$

5. Write the decimal as a sum of a whole number and decimal fractions.
Do not write the fractions with a numerator of 0.

a) $4.017 = \underline{4} + \frac{1}{100} + \frac{7}{1,000}$

b) $8.305 = \underline{} + \frac{}{10} + \frac{}{1,000}$

c) $0.801 =$

d) $9.058 =$

e) $0.005 =$

f) $6.003 =$

6. What is the value of the 9 in each decimal? Write the answer two ways.

a) 0.497 $\frac{9}{100}$ or   _9 hundredths_

b) 8.439 $\frac{9}{}$ or   _9_

c) 1.923 $\frac{9}{}$ or   _____

d) 0.907 $\frac{9}{}$ or   _____

e) 0.749 ——   or   _____

f) 7.591 ——   or   _____

g) 4.903 ——   or   _____

h) 3.809 ——   or   _____

JUMP Math Accumula

7. Write the decimal fraction in the place value chart, then write the number as a decimal.

a) $\dfrac{3}{10} = 0.\underline{\ 3\ }$

Ones	Tenths
0	3

b) $\dfrac{7}{10} = 0.\underline{\ \ \ \ }$

Ones	Tenths

c) $\dfrac{7}{10} + \dfrac{3}{100} = \underline{\ 0\ }.\underline{\ \ \ }\ \underline{\ \ \ }$

Ones	Tenths	Hundredths
0		

d) $\dfrac{3}{10} + \dfrac{8}{100} = \underline{\ \ \ }.\underline{\ \ \ }\ \underline{\ \ \ }$

Ones	Tenths	Hundredths

e) $\dfrac{2}{10} + \dfrac{4}{100} = \underline{\ \ \ }.\underline{\ \ \ }\ \underline{\ \ \ }$

Ones	Tenths	Hundredths
0		

f) $\dfrac{1}{10} + \dfrac{9}{100} + \dfrac{3}{1,000} = \underline{\ \ \ }.\underline{\ \ \ }\ \underline{\ \ \ }\ \underline{\ \ \ }$

Ones	Tenths	Hundredths	Thousandths
0	1	9	3

g) $\dfrac{1}{10} + \dfrac{3}{100} + \dfrac{8}{1,000} = \underline{\ \ \ }.\underline{\ \ \ }\ \underline{\ \ \ }\ \underline{\ \ \ }$

Ones	Tenths	Hundredths	Thousandths
0			

h) $5 + \dfrac{2}{10} + \dfrac{4}{100} = \underline{\ 5\ }.\underline{\ \ \ }\ \underline{\ \ \ }$

Ones	Tenths	Hundredths
5		

i) $7 + \dfrac{5}{100} + \dfrac{3}{1,000} = \underline{\ \ \ }.\underline{\ \ \ }\ \underline{\ \ \ }\ \underline{\ \ \ }$

Ones	Tenths	Hundredths	Thousandths

j) $50 + 8 + \dfrac{1}{100} = \underline{\ \ \ }\ \underline{\ \ \ }.\underline{\ \ \ }\ \underline{\ \ \ }$

Tens	Ones	Tenths	Hundredths

8. The decimal point is between the _____ and _____ place values.

9. Write the decimal in the place value chart.

	Ones	Tenths	Hundredths	Thousandths
a) 0.51	0	5	1	← leave this blank because there are no thousandths in 0.51
b) 0.6	0	6		
c) 0.5				
d) 1.354				
e) 7.482				
f) 0.9				
g) 7.53				

31. Positive and Negative Decimals

The whole-number part of a decimal is the part **to the left** of the decimal point.

decimal point

17.348

whole-number part   fractional part

1. Underline the whole-number part of the decimal.

    a) <u>36</u>.497   b) 807.3   c) 16.54   d) 9.051   e) 0.92

2. Write the number as a decimal.

    a) 3 tens + 6 ones + 2 tenths + 5 hundredths + 3 thousandths = ____ ____.____ ____ ____

    b) 8 ones + 6 tenths + 1 hundredth + 4 thousandths = _____

    c) 6 tens + 9 ones + 7 tenths + 3 hundredths = _____

3. Write the decimal in the place value chart.

	Hundreds	Tens	Ones	Tenths	Hundredths	Thousandths
a) 17.34		1	7	3	4	
b) 9.213						
c) 630.54						
d) 87.006						

4. Write the whole number and how many hundredths or thousandths.

    a) 6.45 ____six____ and ____forty-five____ hundredths

    b) 2.46 _____ and _____ hundredths

    c) 93.005 _____ and _____ thousandths

    d) 5.083 _____ and _____ thousandths

    e) 70.201 _____ and _____ thousandths

5. Write the decimal in words.

    a) 6.8 ____six and eight tenths_____

    b) 6.03 _____

    c) 15.84 _____

    d) 72.359 _____

A decimal can be written as a mixed number. Example: $3.75 = 3\frac{75}{100}$

6. Write the number represented on the grids in three ways.

a)
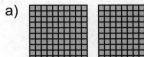

_2_ ones _35_ hundredths   _2_ . _3_ _5_   _2_ $\frac{35}{100}$

b)
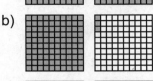

____ one ____ hundredths   ____ . ____ ____   ____$\frac{}{100}$

c)

____ one ____ hundredths   ____ . ____ ____   ____$\frac{}{100}$

7. Write a mixed number for the decimal.

a) $5.3 =$ b) $7.05 =$ c) $6.034 =$

When two numbers are equal, so are their opposites!

Example: $7.4 = 7\frac{4}{10}$ so $-7.4 = -7\frac{4}{10}$

8. Write a negative mixed number for the negative decimal.

a) -3.21 b) -3.85 c) -6.8 d) -1.973 e) -13.67 f) -28.404

$-3\frac{21}{100}$

9. Write a decimal for the mixed number.

a) $+2\frac{13}{100}$ b) $-1\frac{53}{100}$ c) $+76\frac{5}{10}$ d) $-5\frac{304}{1,000}$ e) $-2\frac{9}{10}$ f) $27\frac{9}{1,000}$

When the whole-number part of the decimal is zero, you don't have to write the 0.

Example: 0.25 can be written as .25.

10. Circle the numbers that are equal to five tenths.

a) $\frac{5}{1,000}$ $\frac{5}{10}$ $\frac{5}{100}$ five hundredths   five tens

.05   0.5   0.05   .5   50   500

b) Write four tenths in at least three ways.

To write an improper fraction as a decimal:

$$\frac{43{,}725}{10} = 4{,}372.5$$

1 zero ⟶ 1 digit

$$\frac{43{,}725}{100} = 437.25$$

2 zeros ⟶ 2 digits

$$\frac{43{,}725}{1{,}000} = 43.725$$

3 zeros ⟶ 3 digits

11. Change the improper fraction into a mixed number by shading the correct number of pieces.

a) $\frac{23}{10}$

Mixed number: _____

b) $\frac{34}{10}$

Mixed number: _____

12. Fill in the blanks. Then write the mixed number.

a) $48 \div 10 =$ _____ R _____ so $\frac{48}{10} = 4\frac{8}{10}$

b) $87 \div 10 =$ _____ R _____ so $\frac{87}{10} =$

c) $99 \div 10 =$ _____ R _____ so $\frac{99}{10} =$

d) $342 \div 100 =$ _____ R _____ so $\frac{342}{100} =$

13. Write the improper fraction as a mixed number and then as a decimal.

a) $\frac{23}{10} = \boxed{2\frac{3}{10}} = \underline{\ \ 2.3\ \ }$

b) $\frac{64}{10} = \boxed{} =$ _____

c) $\frac{838}{100} = \boxed{} =$ _____

d) $\frac{9{,}547}{100} = \boxed{} =$ _____

To write the improper fraction $\frac{43{,}725}{100}$ as a decimal:

Step 1: Write the numerator without the commas.

Step 2: Place the decimal point to match the denominator of the fraction.

$$\frac{43{,}725}{100} = 437.25$$

2 zeros   2 digits

14. Write the improper fraction as a decimal.

a) $\frac{74}{10} = \underline{\ \ 7.4\ \ }$

b) $\frac{536}{100} =$ _____

c) $\frac{712}{100} =$ _____

d) $\frac{6{,}347}{10} =$ _____

e) $\frac{2{,}804}{100} =$ _____

Bonus ▶ $\frac{714{,}295}{10{,}000} =$ _____

15. Write the negative improper fraction as a negative decimal.

a) $-\frac{89}{10} = \underline{\ \ -8.9\ \ }$

b) $-\frac{341}{10} =$ _____

c) $-\frac{512}{100} =$ _____

d) $-\frac{608}{10} =$ _____

e) $-\frac{5{,}903}{100} =$ _____

Bonus ▶ $-\frac{643{,}081}{10{,}000} =$ _____

32. Adding and Subtracting Multi-Digit Decimals

1. Add the decimals by adding each place value, then regroup.

a) $0.72 + 4.5$

	Ones	Tenths	Hundredths
+			

← after regrouping →

b) $60.8 + 8.94$

	Tens	Ones	Tenths	Hundredths
+				

2. Add the decimals by lining up the decimal points.

a) $0.32 + 0.57$

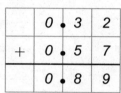

b) $0.61 + 0.03$

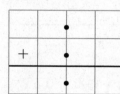

c) $0.6 + 0.27$

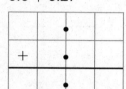

d) $0.31 + 0.48$

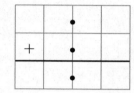

> You can show regrouping on a grid.
>
> Example: $6.9 + 2.3$
>
> 9 tenths + 3 tenths = 12 tenths were regrouped as **1** one and **2** tenths
>
>

3. Add the decimals by lining up the decimal points. You will need to regroup.

a) $0.9 + 0.47$

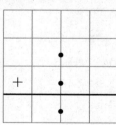

b) $0.68 + 0.37$

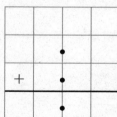

c) $0.91 + 0.59$

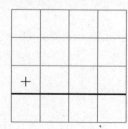

d) $0.35 + 0.23 + 2.47$

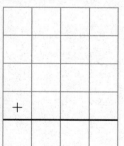

4. Line up the decimal points and add the following numbers.

a) $5.34 + 2.19$ b) $3.68 + 5.43$ c) $4.972 + 3.287$ d) $0.678 + 0.73$

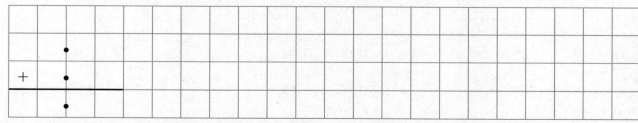

5. Subtract the decimals by lining up the decimal points.

a) 0.53 − 0.21

	0	.	5	3
−	0	.	2	1
	0	.	3	2

b) 0.77 − 0.43

c) 0.58 − 0.21

d) 0.57 − 0.12

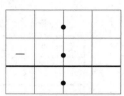

6. Subtract the decimals. You will need to regroup.

a) 0.35 − 0.17

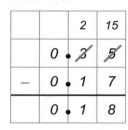

b) 0.84 − 0.58

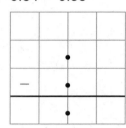

c) 0.82 − 0.49

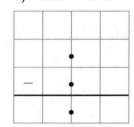

d) 0.73 − 0.49

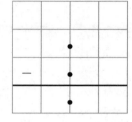

e) 1.00 − 0.73   f) 1.00 − 0.39   g) 1.00 − 0.55   h) 1.00 − 0.92

7. Subtract the decimals.

a) .91 − .45   b) .97 − .59   c) .72 − .57   d) .31 − .24

e) .58 − .2   f) .73 − .7   g) .876 − .014   h) .630 − .182

To add two numbers with the same sign (+ or −), add the absolute values. The sum has the same sign as both numbers.

Example: To add − 3.2 − 4.6, first add 3.2 + 4.6 = 7.8. So − 3.2 − 4.6 = −7.8.

---

8. Use the grid to add the absolute values. Then write the answer with the correct sign.

a) − 3.25 − 18.5

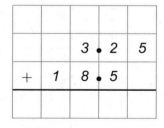

_____

b) + 16.9 + 7.85

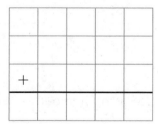

_____

c) − 17.04 − 18.37

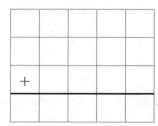

_____

d) + 17.41 + 3.894   e) − 493.1 − 18.4   f) + 3.47 + 1.62

g) − 182.3 − 18.23   h) − 15.3 − 37.49   i) − 5.84 − 71.2 − 18.35

To add two numbers with different signs, subtract their absolute values. The sum has the same sign as the number with the greater absolute value.

Example: To add $-5.2 + 4.6$, subtract $5.2 - 4.6 = 0.6$. Since $|-5.2| > |4.6|$, the sum is negative.
So $-5.2 + 4.6 = -0.6$.

9. Add the numbers by subtracting the absolute values.

a) $-5.8 + 18.93$

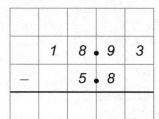

b) $+21.4 - 58.63$

c) $-7.43 + 26.28$

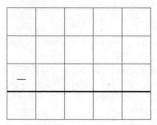

d) $-15.4 + 6.83$ e) $+70.4 - 107.2$ f) $-5.46 + 17.4$

REMINDER: $+(+) = +$ $+(-) = -$ $-(+) = -$ $-(-) = +$

---

10. Rewrite the question. Then add or subtract.

a) $-5.4 - (+3.61)$

$= \underline{\quad -5.4 - 3.61 \quad}$

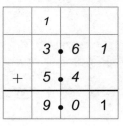

b) $+18.5 + (-4.8)$

$= \underline{\qquad\qquad}$

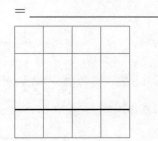

c) $+74.21 - (+8.5)$

$= \underline{\qquad\qquad}$

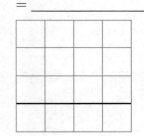

d) $-32.18 - (-5.714)$ e) $+13.61 - (-7.4)$ f) $-5.2 + (+17.63)$

11. A bank statement shows a credit when money is put in and a debit when money is taken out.

a) Complete the balance column.

b) The first debit shown was a mistake by the bank and is cancelled. What is the new bank account balance?

Debit (−)	Credit (+)	Balance
		$0
$15.34		−$15.34
	$27.81	
$23.42		
	$5.41	

33. Division with Fractional and Decimal Answers

Three people share 5 pancakes. How much does each person get?

Divide each pancake into thirds. Give each person one piece from each pancake. The shaded parts show how much one person gets.

Each person gets $\dfrac{1}{3} + \dfrac{1}{3} + \dfrac{1}{3} + \dfrac{1}{3} + \dfrac{1}{3} = 5 \times \dfrac{1}{3} = \dfrac{5}{3}$ pancakes.

1. Shade one person's share of the pancakes. How much does each person get?

a) 5 people share 4 pancakes.

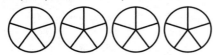

_____ × _____ = _____ pancakes

b) 4 people share 3 pancakes.

_____ × _____ = _____ pancakes

2. Draw a picture to solve the problem: 4 people share 7 oranges.

How many oranges does each person get? _____

The division sign (÷) can be used for equal sharing, whether the answer is a whole number or not.

Example: When 3 people share 5 pancakes equally, each person gets $\dfrac{5}{3}$ pancakes. So, $5 \div 3 = \dfrac{5}{3}$.

3. Draw a picture to show how much one person gets. Write the division equation.

a) Two people share 9 pancakes.

_____ ÷ _____ = _____

b) Four people share 5 pancakes.

_____ ÷ _____ = _____

4. Divide. Write the answer as a fraction and a decimal.

a) $3 \div 10$

$= \dfrac{3}{10}$

$= 0.3$

b) $38 \div 100$

$=$

$=$

c) $53 \div 10$

$=$

$=$

d) $7 \div 1,000$

$=$

$=$

e) $912 \div 10$

$=$

$=$

f) $638 \div 100$

$=$

$=$

g) $49 \div 1,000$

$=$

$=$

h) $30,408 \div 1,000$

$=$

$=$

5. Divide. Write your answer as a decimal.

a) $3 \div 5$

$\dfrac{3}{5} = \dfrac{}{10} = $ _____

b) $7 \div 5$

$\dfrac{7}{5} = \dfrac{}{10} = $ _____

c) $9 \div 20$

$\dfrac{9}{20} = \dfrac{}{100} = $ _____

d) $10 \div 4$

e) $3 \div 4$

f) $28 \div 20$

g) $33 \div 20$

h) $21 \div 25$

i) $7 \div 4$

Bonus ▶ $11 \div 8$

6. Compare your answers to Question 5, parts b) and f). What do you notice? Why is that the case?

34. Long Division

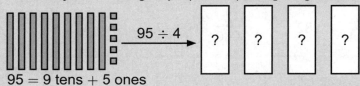

Divide 95 objects into 4 groups (95 ÷ 4) using long division and a base ten model:

95 = 9 tens + 5 ones

Step 1: Write the number like this:

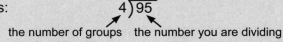

the number of groups   the number you are dividing

Step 2: How can you divide 9 tens blocks equally into the 4 groups?
You can divide 8 of the 9 tens blocks into 4 equal groups of size 2:

There are 2 tens blocks in each group. →
There are 4 groups.
2 × 4 = 8 tens blocks placed →

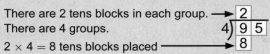

1. How many groups are you going to make? How many tens blocks can you put in each group?

a) $4\overline{)91}$

groups _____

number of tens
in each group _____

b) $3\overline{)84}$

groups _____

number of tens
in each group _____

c) $6\overline{)75}$

groups _____

number of tens
in each group _____

d) $2\overline{)93}$

groups _____

number of tens
in each group _____

2. Find out how many tens can be placed in each group. Then multiply to find out
how many tens have been placed.

a) 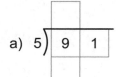   b) 3) 8 2   c) 4) 9 8   d) 5) 9 9   e)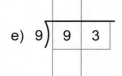

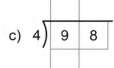

Step 3: How many tens blocks are left?

Subtract to find out. →

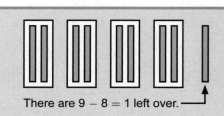

There are 9 − 8 = 1 left over. →

3. For each question, carry out the first three steps of long division.

a) 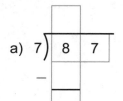   b) 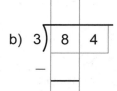   c) 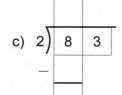   d) 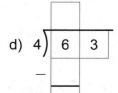   e)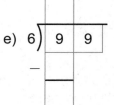

Step 4: There is 1 tens block left over, and there are 5 ones in 95. So there are 15 ones left in total. Write the 5 beside the 1 to show this.

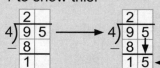

← There are still this many ones to place.

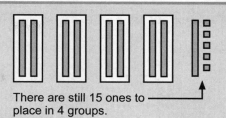

There are still 15 ones to place in 4 groups.

4. Carry out the first four steps of long division.

a) 5)8 5   b) 7)9 7   c) 4)9 2   d) 2)7 5   e) 2)7 3

Step 5: How many ones can you put in each group?

Divide to find out:

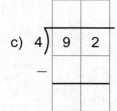 ← 15 ÷ 4 = **3** R ___

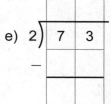

How many ones are left over? ?

5. Carry out the first five steps of long division.

a) 5)6 1   b) 4)4 7   c) 2)8 6   d) 3)6 3   e) 5)8 1

Step 6 and 7: Find the number of ones left over.

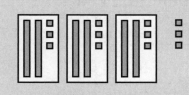

```
    2 3
  4)9 5
  − 8
    1 5
  − 1 2   ← There are 3 × 4 = 12 ones placed.
      3   ← There are 15 − 12 = 3 ones left over.
```

Long division and the model both show that **95 ÷ 4 = 23 with 3 left over**.

6. Carry out all the steps of long division on grid paper.

a) 6)81   b) 4)52   c) 3)95   d) 3)82   e) 4)64

f) 7)87   g) 6)92   h) 8)90   i) 9)84   j) 9)71

To divide 334 objects into 2 groups using long division:

Step 1: Divide the hundreds into 2 groups.

```
      1
  2) 3 3 4
   - 2
     1
```

Step 2: Regroup the remaining hundreds as tens.

```
      1
  2) 3 3 4
   - 2
     1 3
```

Step 3: Divide the tens into 2 groups.

```
      1 6
  2) 3 3 4
   - 2
     1 3
   - 1 2
       1
```

Step 4: Regroup the remaining tens as ones and divide.

```
      1 6 7
  2) 3 3 4
   - 2
     1 3
   - 1 2
       1 4
     - 1 4
         0
```

7. Divide.

a) 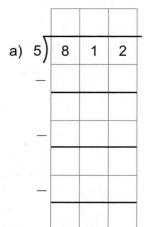 5) 8 1 2

b) 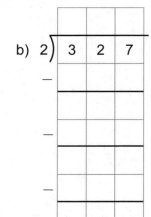 2) 3 2 7

c) 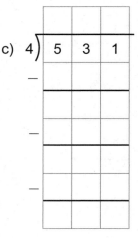 4) 5 3 1

d) 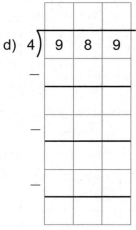 4) 9 8 9

REMINDER: You can write division answers as decimals instead of with a remainder.

Example: $16 \div 5 = 3\ R\ 1$, so $16 \div 5 = 3\frac{1}{5} = 3\frac{2}{10} = 3.2$

8. Write your answers to Question 7 as decimals.

a) $812 \div 5 = $ _____

b) $327 \div 2 = $ _____

c) $531 \div 4 = $ _____

d) $989 \div 4 = $ _____

9. Divide using long division. Write your answers as decimals.

a) $917 \div 5$

b) $577 \div 2$

c) $794 \div 4$

d) $895 \div 4$

e) $811 \div 2$

f) $614 \div 4$

g) $836 \div 5$

h) $981 \div 8$

10. In each question below, there are not enough tens to divide into the groups. Write a "0" in the tens place to show that no tens can be placed, then continue the division, regrouping tens as ones.

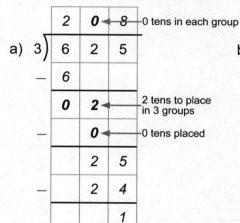

a) and the worked example showing:

2 0 ← 8 — 0 tens in each group
3)6 2 5
− 6
0 2 ← 2 tens to place in 3 groups
− 0 ← 0 tens placed
2 5
− 2 4
1

b) 4)8 1 7   c) 2)6 1 7      d) 7)7 6 1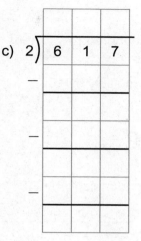

11. In each question below, there are fewer hundreds than the number of groups. Write a "0" in the hundreds place to show that no hundreds can be placed in equal groups. Then perform the division as if the hundreds had been exchanged for tens.

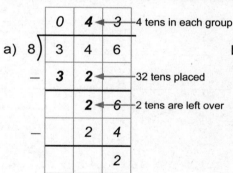

a) worked example:

0 4 ← 3 — 4 tens in each group
8)3 4 6
− 3 2 ← 32 tens placed
2 ← 6 — 2 tens are left over
− 2 4
2

b) 5)3 9 5   c) 9)6 9 6   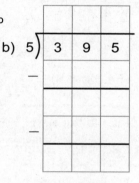   d) 7)5 1 8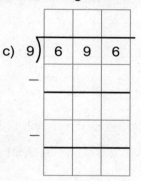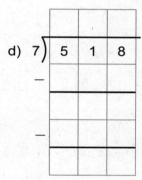

e) 3)121   f) 4)214   g) 8)641   h) 6)584   i) 9)365

12. In each question below, say how many tens or hundreds can be placed in 5 groups. Underline the place values you will divide by 5.

a) 5)315   b) 5)726   c) 5)623   d) 5)321

_____31 tens_____   _____7 hundreds_____   _____   _____

e) 5)892   f) 5)240   g) 5)987   h) 5)412

_____   _____   _____   _____

13. Divide. Write your answer as a decimal.

a) 2)136   b) 4)263   c) 5)584   d) 5)407

e) 2)7,913   f) 4)9,807   g) 5)2,764   h) 8)4,012

35. Multiplying Decimals by Powers of 10

REMINDER: Each place value is 10 times greater than the place value to its right.

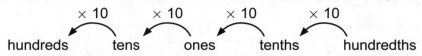

× 10 × 10 × 10 × 10

hundreds   tens   ones   tenths   hundredths

1. Use place value to multiply by 10.

   a) 3 tens × 10

   = ___3 hundreds___

   b) 5 hundredths × 10

   = _____

   c) 8 tenths × 10

   = _____

2. Use expanded form to multiply by 10.

   a) 24.7 = ___20 + 4 + 0.7___ so 24.7 × 10 = ___200 + 40 + 7___ = ___247___

   b) 7.12 = _____ so 7.12 × 10 = _____ = _____

   c) 0.345 = _____ so 0.345 × 10 = _____ = _____

   d) 16.4 = _____ so 16.4 × 10 = _____ = _____

   e) 0.803 = _____ so 0.803 × 10 = _____ = _____

   f) 54.03 = _____ so 54.03 × 10 = _____ = _____

To multiply by 10, shift the decimal point one place to the right.

To multiply by 100, shift the decimal point two places to the right.

3. Multiply by 10 or 100. Do your rough work in the grid.

   a) 100 × 0.7 = ___70___

   | 0 . | 7 | | |

   | | 7 | 0 . | |

   b) 10 × 3.6 = _____

   c) 0.045 × 10 = _____

   d) 8.9 × 100 = _____

   e) 0.704 × 100 = _____

   f) 6.84 × 10 = _____

   g) 3.081 × 10 = _____

   h) 0.051 × 100 = _____

4. Change the fraction equation to a decimal equation and write how many places the decimal point moved.

a) $1{,}000 \times \dfrac{1}{1{,}000} = 1$

so ___1,000___ × ___0.001___ = ___1___

The decimal point moved ___3___ places right.

b) $100{,}000 \times \dfrac{1}{100{,}000} = 1$

so _____ × _____ = _____

The decimal point moved _____ places right.

c) $10{,}000 \times \dfrac{1}{10{,}000} = 1$

so _____ × _____ = _____

The decimal point moved _____ places right.

d) $10{,}000{,}000 \times \dfrac{1}{10{,}000{,}000} = 1$

so _____ × _____ = _____

The decimal point moved _____ places right.

5. To multiply by a power of 10 (such as 10, 100, 1,000, and so on), shift the decimal point the correct number of places to the right.

a) $1{,}000 \times 0.076 =$ _____

b) $1{,}000 \times 5.03 \; =$ _____

c) $3.8 \times 100 \quad =$ _____

d) $0.07 \times 10{,}000 \quad =$ _____

e) $100{,}000 \times 0.00004 \quad =$ _____

f) $0.0081 \times 1{,}000{,}000 \quad =$ _____

6. To change from centimeters to millimeters, you multiply by 10. There are 10 mm in 1 cm. Convert the centimeters to millimeters.

a) 5.3 cm = _____ mm   b) 0.16 cm = _____ mm   c) 80 cm = _____ mm

7. A quarter is 0.175 cm thick. How tall would a stack of 100 quarters be? _____

8. To multiply by 10,000,000,000, move the decimal point _____ places to the right.

9. Skip count by 0.4s to multiply 10 × 0.4.

36. Multiplying and Dividing by Powers of 10

> Division can be used to "undo" multiplication. $4 \xrightarrow{\times 3} 12$ and $12 \xrightarrow{\div 3} 4$

1. How do you undo multiplying by 10, 100, or 1,000?

   a) To multiply by 10, I move the decimal point _____ place to the _____.

      So, to divide by 10, I move the decimal point _____ place to the _____.

   b) To multiply by 100, I move the decimal point _____ places to the _____.

      So, to divide by 100, I move the decimal point _____ places to the _____.

   c) To multiply by 1,000, I move the decimal point _____ places to the _____.

      So, to divide by 1,000, I move the decimal point _____ places to the _____.

2. Divide by shifting the decimal point one, two, or three places to the left.

   a) $0.7 \div 10$ =   _____

   b) $52.3 \div 1,000$ =   _____

   c) $7.5 \div 1,000$ =   _____

   d) $8.9 \div 100$ =   _____

   e) $36,543.26 \div 1,000$ =   _____

   If there is no decimal point, add one to the right of the number first.

   f) $80 \div 100$ =   _____

   g) $9 \div 10$ =   _____

   h) $2,543,700 \div 1,000$ =   _____

3. Explain why $1.00 \div 100 = 0.01$. Use a dollar bill as the whole.

4. A 3.6 m wide wall is painted with 100 stripes of equal width. How wide is each strip?

5. a) To multiply by 10, move the decimal point ____1____ place(s) to the _____.

b) To divide by 1,000, move the decimal point _____ place(s) to the _____.

c) To multiply by 100, move the decimal point _____ place(s) to the _____.

d) To _____ by 10, move the decimal point _____ place(s) to the left.

e) To _____ by 1,000, move the decimal point _____ place(s) to the right.

f) To divide by _____, move the decimal point 2 places to the _____.

g) To multiply by _____, move the decimal point 4 places to the _____.

h) To multiply by 100,000, move the decimal point _____ place(s) to the _____.

i) To divide by 10,000,000, move the decimal point _____ place(s) to the _____.

6. Fill in the blanks. Next, draw arrows to show how you would shift the decimal point. Then write your final answer in the grid.

a) $7.845 \times 1,000$

Move the decimal point _____ places _____.

b) $5.4 \div 100$

Move the decimal point _____ places _____.

c) $247.567 \times 10,000$

Move the decimal point _____ places _____.

d) $100.45 \div 10,000$

Move the decimal point _____ places _____.

e) $0.602 \times 100,000$ f) $24.682 \div 10,000$ g) $0.07 \times 100,000$ h) $36.07 \div 1,000$

7. a) Multiply the fraction by 10. Write your answer in lowest terms.

i) $10 \times \dfrac{2}{10}$ ii) $10 \times \dfrac{3}{100}$ iii) $10 \times \dfrac{16}{10}$ iv) $10 \times \dfrac{7}{1,000}$

b) Multiply the decimal by 10.

i) 10×0.2 ii) 10×0.03 iii) 10×1.6 iv) 10×0.007

c) Are your answers to parts a) and b) the same? Why is this the case?

37. Multiplying Decimals by Whole Numbers

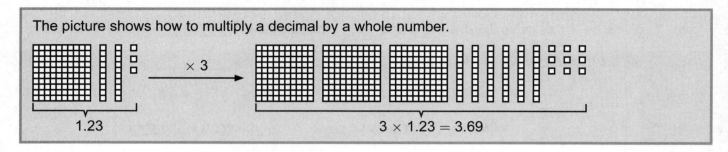

The picture shows how to multiply a decimal by a whole number.

1.23   × 3   3 × 1.23 = 3.69

1. Multiply mentally. Multiply each digit separately.

   a) $3 \times 2.13 =$ _____   b) $2 \times 4.2 =$ _____   c) $8 \times 1.01 =$ _____   d) $3 \times 2.3 =$ _____

   e) $4 \times 2.21 =$ _____   f) $3 \times 1.3 =$ _____   g) $3 \times 4.21 =$ _____   h) $8 \times 4.11 =$ _____

2. Multiply by exchanging tenths for ones.

   a) $7 \times 1.3 =$ __7__ ones + __21__ tenths   b) $3 \times 3.6 =$ _____ ones + _____ tenths

   $\quad\quad\quad = $ __9__ ones + __1__ tenth $\quad\quad\quad = $ _____ ones + _____ tenths

   $\quad\quad\quad = $ __9.1__ $\quad\quad\quad = $ _____

   c) $11 \times 1.2 =$ __11__ ones + __22__ tenths   d) $12 \times 4.2 =$ _____ ones + _____ tenths

   $\quad\quad\quad = $ _____ ones + _____ tenths $\quad\quad\quad = $ _____ ones + _____ tenths

   $\quad\quad\quad = $ _____ $\quad\quad\quad = $ _____

3. Multiply by exchanging tenths for ones or hundredths for tenths.

   a) $3 \times 3.15 =$ _____ ones + _____ tenths + _____ hundredths

   $\quad\quad\quad = $ _____ ones + _____ tenths + _____ hundredths $=$ _____

   b) $4 \times 2.41 =$ _____ ones + _____ tenths + _____ hundredths

   $\quad\quad\quad = $ _____ ones + _____ tenths + _____ hundredths $=$ _____

   You may need to regroup twice.

   c) $4 \times 1.34 =$ _____ ones + _____ tenths + _____ hundredths

   $\quad\quad\quad = $ _____ ones + _____ tenths + _____ hundredths

   $\quad\quad\quad = $ _____ ones + _____ tenths + _____ hundredths $=$ _____

   d) $11 \times 2.13 =$ _____ ones + _____ tenths + _____ hundredths

   $\quad\quad\quad = $ _____ ones + _____ tenths + _____ hundredths

   $\quad\quad\quad = $ _____ ones + _____ tenths + _____ hundredths $=$ _____

To multiply a decimal and a whole number:

Step 1: Multiply as though both numbers are whole numbers.

Step 2: In the product of the whole numbers, put as many digits after the decimal point as the decimal has. Remove any final 0s.

Example: 3.42×15

$342 \times 15 = 5{,}130$

$3.42 \times 15 = 51.30$

$ = 51.3$

This works because 342×15 is 100 times greater than 3.42×15.

4. Multiply. In some questions you will have to regroup twice.

a)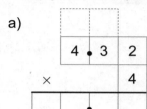

b)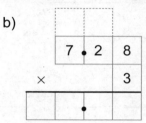

c)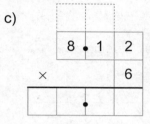

d)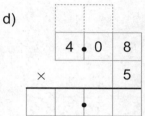

e)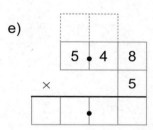

f)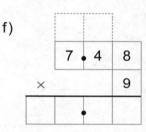

g)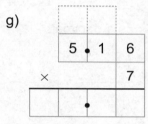

h)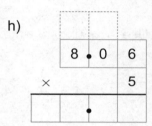

i) 5×3.6

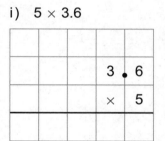

j) 3×0.4

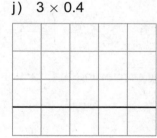

k) 4.2×6

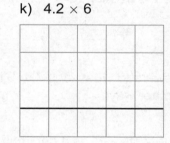

l) 3×46.92

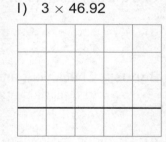

5. Multiply.

a)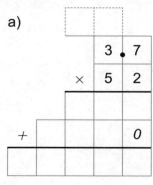

b)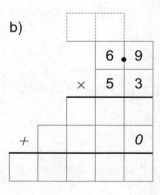

c)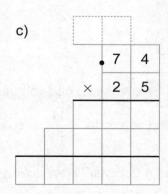

d)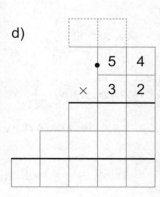

e) 13×2.3

f) 4.2×15

g) 4×36.75

h) 21×18.04

6. Multiply by using repeated addition.

a) $2 \times 0.8 = $ _____ = _____

b) $3 \times (-0.6) = $ _____ = _____

c) $3 \times 1.3 = $ _____ = _____

d) $2 \times (-1.8) = $ _____ = _____

e) $7 \times (-2.1) = $ _____ = _____

7. Use $\dfrac{1}{5} = 0.2$ to write $\dfrac{4}{5}$ as a decimal.

$$\frac{4}{5} = \frac{1}{5} + \frac{1}{5} + \frac{1}{5} + \frac{1}{5} = \underline{\ 0.2\ } + \underline{\hspace{1cm}} + \underline{\hspace{1cm}} + \underline{\hspace{1cm}} = \underline{\hspace{1cm}}$$

8. Use $\dfrac{1}{4} = 0.25$ to write $-\dfrac{3}{4}$ as a decimal.

$$-\frac{3}{4} = -\frac{1}{4} - \frac{1}{4} - \frac{1}{4} = -\underline{\hspace{1cm}} - \underline{\hspace{1cm}} - \underline{\hspace{1cm}} = \underline{\hspace{1cm}}$$

9. Use multiplication to write the fraction as a decimal.

a) $\dfrac{3}{2} = 3 \times \dfrac{1}{2} = 3 \times \underline{\hspace{1cm}} = \underline{\hspace{1cm}}$

b) $-\dfrac{5}{4} = 5 \times \left(-\dfrac{1}{4}\right) = 5 \times (\underline{\hspace{1cm}}) = \underline{\hspace{1cm}}$

Bonus ▶ Check your answers to Questions 7 to 9 by converting the fractions to decimals another way.

10. a) Continue the pattern to write $\dfrac{7}{20}$ as a decimal.

$\dfrac{1}{20}$	$\dfrac{2}{20}$	$\dfrac{3}{20}$	$\dfrac{4}{20}$	$\dfrac{5}{20}$	$\dfrac{6}{20}$	$\dfrac{7}{20}$
0.05	0.10	0.15	0.20	_____	_____	_____

b) If you know $\dfrac{1}{20}$ as a decimal, how can you use multiplication to write $\dfrac{11}{20}$ as a decimal? How can you write $-\dfrac{11}{20}$ as a decimal?

c) What is $\dfrac{17}{20}$ written as a decimal? How does your answer compare to $\dfrac{7}{20}$ as a decimal? Why does this make sense?

38. Percentages

A **percentage** is a ratio that compares a number to 100.

The term *percent* means "per 100" or "for every 100" or "out of 100." For example, 84% on a test means 84 out of 100.

You can think of a percentage as a short form for a fraction with denominator 100. Example: $45\% = \dfrac{45}{100}$

1. Write the percentage as a fraction.

    a) 3%
    b) 87%
    c) 6%
    d) 35%

    e) 50%
    f) 100%
    g) 9%
    h) 13%

2. Write the fraction as a percentage.

    a) $\dfrac{2}{100}$
    b) $\dfrac{13}{100}$
    c) $\dfrac{27}{100}$
    d) $\dfrac{100}{100}$

    e) $\dfrac{19}{100}$
    f) $\dfrac{66}{100}$
    g) $\dfrac{8}{100}$
    h) $\dfrac{1}{100}$

3. Write the decimal as a fraction and then a percentage.

    a) $0.72 = \dfrac{72}{100} = 72\%$
    b) 0.34
    c) 0.05

4. Write the fraction as a percentage by first changing it to a fraction with denominator 100.

    a) $\dfrac{3 \times 20}{5 \times 20} = \dfrac{60}{100} = 60\%$
    b) $\dfrac{2}{5}$

    c) $\dfrac{4}{5}$
    d) $\dfrac{1}{4}$

    e) $\dfrac{3}{4}$
    f) $\dfrac{1}{2}$

    g) $\dfrac{1}{10}$
    h) $\dfrac{9}{10}$

    i) $\dfrac{19}{25}$
    j) $\dfrac{13}{20}$

    k) $\dfrac{7}{25}$
    l) $\dfrac{15}{20}$

    m) $\dfrac{43}{50}$
    n) $\dfrac{27}{50}$

5. Write the decimal as a percentage.

a) $0.2 = \dfrac{2 \times 10}{10 \times 10} = \dfrac{20}{100} = 20\%$

b) 0.5

c) 0.7

d) 0.9

6. Write the percentage as a fraction, then as a decimal.

a) $32\% = \dfrac{32}{100} = 0.32$

b) 8%

c) 51%

d) 4%

7. What percent of the figure is shaded?

a)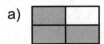

b)

c)

d)

8. Change the fraction to a percentage by first reducing it to lowest terms.

a) $\dfrac{9 \div 3}{15 \div 3} = \dfrac{3}{5} = \dfrac{3 \times 20}{5 \times 20} = \dfrac{60}{100} = 60\%$

b) $\dfrac{12}{15}$

c) $\dfrac{3}{6}$

d) $\dfrac{14}{35}$

e) $\dfrac{21}{28}$

f) $\dfrac{11}{44}$

g) $\dfrac{24}{30}$

h) $\dfrac{8}{16}$

i) $\dfrac{30}{40}$

j) $\dfrac{8}{40}$

k) $\dfrac{90}{150}$

l) $\dfrac{45}{75}$

39. Decimals, Fractions, and Percentages

1. Fill in the chart. The first column has been done for you.

Drawing				
Fraction	$\dfrac{23}{100}$	$\dfrac{\ \ \ }{100}$	$\dfrac{54}{100}$	$\dfrac{\ \ \ }{100}$
Decimal	0.23	0._____	0._____	0.87
Percent	23%	36%	_____%	_____%

2. Use a centimeter ruler. Color 50% of the rectangle blue, $\dfrac{4}{10}$ red, and 0.1 green.

3. Write the shaded part in three ways.

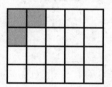

Fraction: _____   Percent: _____   Decimal: _____

4. Write a fraction and a percentage for each division of the number line.

a)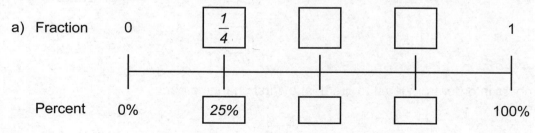

b)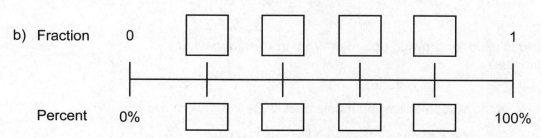

5. Complete the chart.

Fraction	$\frac{1}{4}$		$\frac{3}{20}$			$\frac{6}{15}$	$\frac{23}{25}$		
Decimal		0.35			0.60				0.55
Percent				30%				75%	

6. Write $<$, $>$, or $=$ between each pair of numbers. Change the numbers in each pair to fractions with the same denominator first.

a) $\frac{1}{2}$ ☐ 47%

$\frac{50 \times 1}{50 \times 2}$ ☐ $\frac{47}{100}$

$\frac{50}{100}$ $\boxed{>}$ $\frac{47}{100}$

b) $\frac{1}{2}$ ☐ 49%

☐

☐

c) $\frac{3}{4}$ ☐ 78%

☐

☐

d) $\frac{2}{5}$ ☐ 35%

☐

☐

e) $\frac{2}{3}$ ☐ 60%

$\frac{100 \times 2}{100 \times 3}$ ☐ $\frac{60 \times 3}{100 \times 3}$

$\frac{200}{300}$ $\boxed{>}$ $\frac{180}{300}$

f) 0.9 ☐ $\frac{8}{9}$

☐

☐

g) 11% ☐ $\frac{1}{9}$

☐

☐

h) $\frac{1}{11}$ ☐ 0.09

☐

☐

i) 0.76 ☐ 93%

☐

☐

j) $\frac{4}{7}$ ☐ 53%

☐

☐

k) 0.7 ☐ 7%

☐

☐

l) 0.9 ☐ 10%

☐

☐

7. Write the set of numbers in order from least to greatest by first changing each number to a fraction.

a) $\frac{3}{5}$, 42%, 0.73

b) $\frac{1}{2}$, 0.74, 80%

c) $\frac{1}{4}$, 0.09, 15%

d) $\frac{2}{3}$, 57%, 0.62

8. 20 m² of a 50 m² field is used for growing potatoes. What fraction and what percent of the field is this?

9. In Sandy's class, 41% of the students like pop music best, 19% like rock music, and $\frac{2}{5}$ like rap music. Which type of music do more students like best?

40. Finding Percentages (Introduction)

If you use a thousands cube to represent 1 whole, you can see that taking $\frac{1}{10}$ of a number is the same as dividing the number by 10—the decimal shifts one place left.

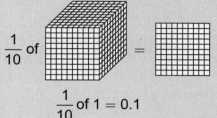

$$\frac{1}{10} \text{ of } 1 = 0.1 \qquad \frac{1}{10} \text{ of } 0.1 = 0.01 \qquad \frac{1}{10} \text{ of } 0.01 = 0.001$$

1. Find $\frac{1}{10}$ of the number by shifting the decimal. Write your answer in the box.

a) 4 (= 4.0)   b) 9   c) 23   d) 210   e) 8.3   f) 5.2

$\boxed{0.4}$ $\boxed{}$ $\boxed{}$ $\boxed{}$ $\boxed{}$ $\boxed{}$

2. 10% is short for $\frac{10}{100}$ or $\frac{1}{10}$. Find 10% of the number.

a) 8   b) 7.5   c) 3.06   d) 6.45   e) 0.09   f) 12.2

$\boxed{}$ $\boxed{}$ $\boxed{}$ $\boxed{}$ $\boxed{}$ $\boxed{}$

You can find percentages that are multiples of 10.

Example: To find 30% of 21, find 10% of 21 and multiply the result by 3.

Step 1: 10% of 21 = $\boxed{2.1}$

Step 2: 3 × $\boxed{2.1}$ = 6.3 $\longrightarrow$ 30% of 21 = 6.3

3. Find the percentage using the method above.

a) 60% of 15

10% of __15__ = $\boxed{}$

__6__ × $\boxed{}$ = _____

b) 80% of 25

10% of _____ = $\boxed{}$

_____ × $\boxed{}$ = _____

c) 90% of 2.3

10% of _____ = $\boxed{}$

_____ × $\boxed{}$ = _____

d) 70% of 35

10% of _____ = $\boxed{}$

_____ × $\boxed{}$ = _____

e) 20% of 24

10% of _____ = $\boxed{}$

_____ × $\boxed{}$ = _____

f) 30% of 1.3

10% of _____ = $\boxed{}$

_____ × $\boxed{}$ = _____

4. Use the number line to fill in the blank.

```
0      4      8      12     16     20     24     28     32     36     40
├──────┼──────┼──────┼──────┼──────┼──────┼──────┼──────┼──────┼──────┤
0%    10%    20%    30%    40%    50%    60%    70%    80%    90%   100%
```

a) 20% of 40 is _____

b) 50% of 40 is _____

c) 85% of 40 is _____

d) 15% of 40 is _____

e) _____% of 40 is 12

f) _____% of 40 is 18

5. A class wrote a science test with 40 possible marks. Help the teacher record the grades as percentages.

a) $\frac{32}{40}$ = _____%

b) $\frac{38}{40}$ = _____%

c) $\frac{14}{40}$ = _____%

d) $\frac{20}{40}$ = _____%

e) $\frac{22}{40}$ = _____%

Bonus ▶ $\frac{21}{40}$ = _____%

6. Use the number line to find 5%, 15%, and 65%.

a)
```
0     50    100   150   200   250   300   350   400   450   500
├──────┼──────┼──────┼──────┼──────┼──────┼──────┼──────┼──────┼──────┤
0%    10%    20%    30%    40%    50%    60%    70%    80%    90%   100%
```

5% of 500 is _____   15% of 500 is _____   65% of 500 is _____

b)
```
0      3      6      9      12     15     18     21     24     27     30
├──────┼──────┼──────┼──────┼──────┼──────┼──────┼──────┼──────┼──────┤
0%    10%    20%    30%    40%    50%    60%    70%    80%    90%   100%
```

5% of 30 is _____   15% of 30 is _____   65% of 30 is _____

c) You will need to finish the number line yourself.

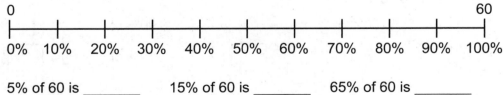
```
0                                                              60
├──────┼──────┼──────┼──────┼──────┼──────┼──────┼──────┼──────┼──────┤
0%    10%    20%    30%    40%    50%    60%    70%    80%    90%   100%
```

5% of 60 is _____   15% of 60 is _____   65% of 60 is _____

7. In Question 6, why should your answers to part c) be double your answers to part b)?

8. At a restaurant, Ted wants to tip the waiter 15%. If his meal cost $30, how much tip should he leave?

9. A bike costs $500. A 5% tax is added. How much is the tax?

41. More Percentages

35% is short for $\dfrac{35}{100}$. To find 35% of 27, Marta finds $\dfrac{35}{100}$ of 27.

Step 1: She multiplies 27 by 35.

```
  2 3
    2 7
  × 3 5
  1 3 5
  8 1 0
  9 4 5
```

Step 2: She divides the result by 100.

$$945 \div 100 = 9.45$$

So 35% of 27 is 9.45.

1. Find the percentage using Marta's method.

a) 25% of 44

   Step 1:
   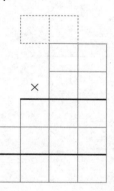

   Step 2: _____ ÷ 100 = _____

   So _____ of _____ is _____.

b) 18% of 92

   Step 1:
   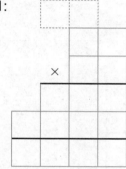

   Step 2: _____ ÷ 100 = _____

   So _____ of _____ is _____.

c) 18% of 95

   Step 1:
   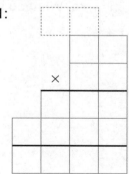

   Step 2: _____ ÷ 100 = _____

   So _____ of _____ is _____.

d) 26% of 84

   Step 1:
   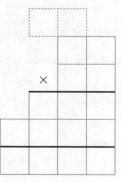

   Step 2: _____ ÷ 100 = _____

   So _____ of _____ is _____.

2. Find the percentage using Marta's method.

   a) 23% of 23   b) 15% of 26   c) 26% of 15   d) 64% of 58

   e) 58% of 64   f) 50% of 81   g) 81% of 50   h) 92% of 11

Amy says 35% is short for 0.35. To find 35% of 27, she multiplies 0.35 × 27.

3. Use Amy's method to find the percentage of the number.

a) 23% of 47 = 0.23 × 47 = _____

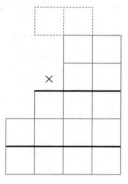

b) 92% of 49 = 0.92 × 49 = _____

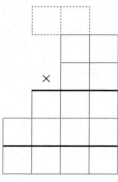

c) 11% of 70 = _____ = _____

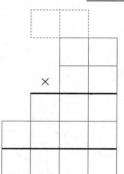

d) 18% of 30 = _____ = _____

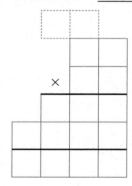

4. a) Find 18% of 23 using two methods:

   i) by writing 18% as a decimal

   ii) by writing 18% as a fraction

   b) In what ways are the methods the same?

5. Calculate 13% of 72 and 72% of 13.

   Compare your answers. What do you notice?

   Why is this the case?

6. a) Calculate 24% of 32.

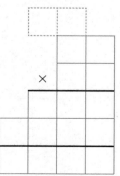

   b) Is your answer more or less than $\frac{1}{4}$ of 32? Why does this make sense?

42. Mental Math and Percentages

You can calculate 25% of a number by dividing the number by 4 because $25\% = \dfrac{25}{100} = \dfrac{1}{4}$.

Examples: 25% of 80 is $\dfrac{1}{4}$ of $80 = 80 \div 4 = 20$.

1. Calculate 25% of the number. Do your rough work in your notebook.

   a) 25% of 60 = _____
   b) 25% of 300 = _____
   c) 25% of 40 = _____

   d) 25% of 30 = _____
   e) 25% of 70 = _____
   f) 25% of 90 = _____

   Bonus ▶ 25% of 1,000,000 = _____

You can add and subtract percentages the same way you add and subtract fractions.

Example: $\dfrac{10}{100} + \dfrac{5}{100} = \dfrac{15}{100}$ so 10% + 5% = 15%.

2. Add or subtract the percentages.

   a) 20% + 5% = _____
   b) 30% + 20% = _____
   c) 10% + 10% = _____

   d) 20% − 5% = _____
   e) 50% − 20% = _____
   f) 75% − 10% = _____

To find 5% of a number, first find 10% of the number, then divide by 2.

To find 20% of a number, first find 10% of the number, then multiply by 2.

3. Complete the chart. Start by finding 10% of each number. Make sure your answers agree with your answers to Question 1.

		60	300	40	30	70	90	Bonus ▶ 1,000,000
a)	5%	3			$\dfrac{3}{2} = 1.5$			
b)	10%	6	30		3			
c)	20%	12						
d)	25% = 20% + 5%	15						

4. 10% of a number is 3. What is the number? _____
   Hint: The number is 100% of the number.

5. Mike wants to leave a 15% tip on a meal that cost $40. How much tip should he leave? _____
Hint: 15% = 10% + 5%

6. Change the fraction to a percentage. Then find the percentage of the stamp collection that comes from other countries.

a) Anne's collection:

USA	Canada	Other
40%	$\frac{1}{2}$	$\frac{1}{10}$
= 40%	= 50%	= 10%

b) Brian's collection:

USA	England	Other
80%	$\frac{1}{10}$	

c) Juan's collection:

USA	Mexico	Other
$\frac{1}{2}$	40%	

7. Calculate the percentages mentally, then add them.

a) 20% of 40 is _____ and 80% of 40 is _____, so 20% of 40 + 80% of 40 is _____.

b) 25% of 32 is _____ and 75% of 32 is _____, so 25% of 32 + 75% of 32 is _____.

c) 40% of 300 is _____ and 60% of 300 is _____, so 40% of 300 + 60% of 300 is _____.

d) 30% of 12 is _____ and 70% of 12 is _____, so 30% of 12 + 70% of 12 is _____.

8. Is 100% of each number in Question 7 equal to the number? If not, find your mistake.

9. a) Find 35% of 40 in two ways. Do you get the same answer both ways?

   i) 35% of 40 = 35 × 40 ÷ 100 = _____ ÷ 100 = _____

   ii) 35% of 40 = 25% of 40 + 10% of 40 = _____ + _____ = _____

   b) 35% is less than 50% or $\frac{1}{2}$. Is your answer to part a) less than half of 40?

   c) Is 35% closer to 0 or to $\frac{1}{2}$? _____

   Was your answer to part a) closer to 0 or to half of 40? _____

   d) Is your answer to part a) reasonable? Explain.

10. Vicky wants to save 25% of her earnings and spend the rest. If she earns $120 a month, how much can she spend each month? _____

11. Jim wants to buy a $400 bike. There is a 5% tax.

   a) How much will he pay in taxes? _____

   b) How much will he pay altogether? _____

JUMP Math Accumula

43. Word Problems

1. Cathy buys a tennis racket worth $80. The tax is 7%.

   How much is the tax? _____

2. Anwar wants to leave a 15% tip on a meal that cost $24.

   How much tip should he leave? _____

> To encourage sales, stores often pay their salespeople **commission**—a percentage of the price of the item that was sold.

3. If a salesperson receives 3% commission, how much would she receive on the sale?

	Item	Price	Commission Amount
a)	CD	$24	$0.72
b)	House	$200,000	
c)	Sweater	$60	
d)	Jacket	$300	

4. Subtract the discount to find the sale price.

	Item	Regular Price	Discount (percent)	Discount ($ amount)	Sale Price
a)	Gloves	$36.00	10%	$3.60	$36.00 − $3.60 = $32.40
b)	Shoes	$49.92	25%		
c)	CD	$14.90	30%		
d)	DVD	$18.50	20%		

5. May's rent will increase by 2% next year. So will her salary.

   a) If her rent is $500 per month this year, how much will her rent increase be in dollars?

   b) How much will her new rent be?

   c) If her salary is $40,000 this year, how much will her salary increase be in dollars?

   d) How much will her new salary be?

6. Don bought cans of juice for 80¢ each. He raises the price by 20%, then sells the cans. How much does he sell each can for?

A car salesperson gets a 30% commission based on the **profit** on the sale.

Example: If a car is bought for $18,000 and sold for $20,000, the commission is …

30% of $2,000 = $600

$20,000 − $18,000

7. Use 30% commission to calculate the amount the car salesperson gets for the sale.

	Car	Buying Price of Car	Selling Price of Car	Profit	Commission Amount
a)	Sedan	$20,000	$24,000	*$4,000*	*$1,200*
b)	Compact car	$15,000	$15,600		
c)	SUV	$43,500	$49,900		
d)	Sports car	$185,000	$197,000		
e)	Pick-up truck	$28,000	$33,000		

8. In the 2012 US presidential election, about 58% of American citizens who were old enough to vote actually voted.

a) What percent of American citizens who were old enough to vote didn't vote?

b) If there were 224,000,000 American citizens who were old enough to vote, how many didn't vote?

9. a) A sweater that usually costs $80 is on sale for 25% off. What is the sale price?

b) How would you estimate the price of a $32.99 shirt that is on sale for 25% off? Hint: 32.99 is close to 32, a multiple of 4.

44. Tape Diagrams, Fractions, and Percentage Problems

1. What percent and what fraction of the whole is each block?

a) ☐☐☐☐☐ $\frac{1}{5}$ = ___20%___   b) ☐☐☐☐ ☐ = _____

c) ☐☐☐☐☐☐☐☐☐☐ ☐ = _____

2. What percent of A is each block? What percent of A is B?

a) A: | 20% | | | | |

    B: | 20% | 20% |

    B is __40__% of A.

b) A: ☐☐☐☐

    B: ☐☐☐

    B is _____% of A.

c) A: ☐☐☐☐☐

    B: ☐☐

    B is _____% of A.

d) A: ☐☐

    B: ☐

    B is _____% of A.

> Sometimes, B is more than A. Then B is more than 100% of A.
>
> Example: 25% of A
>
>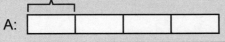
>
> A: ☐☐☐☐
>
> B: ☐☐☐☐☐
>
> 125% of A

3. What percent of A is B?

a) A: ☐☐☐☐

    B: ☐☐☐☐☐☐

   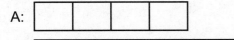

    B is _____% of A.

b) A: ☐☐

    B: ☐☐☐

   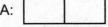

    B is _____% of A.

c) A: ☐

    B: ☐☐☐

    B is _____% of A.

d) A: ☐☐

    B: ☐☐☐☐

    B is _____% of A.

4. What percent of the total is A?

a) A: [box divided into 2]

   B: [box divided into 3]

   A is _____% of the total.

b) A: [1 box]

   B: [box divided into 9]

   A is _____% of the total.

c) A: [box divided into 3]

   B: [1 box]

   A is _____% of the total.

d) A: [box divided into 3]

   B: [box divided into 6]

   A is _____% of the total.

Bonus ▶ A: [box divided into 7]

   B: [1 box]

   C: [box divided into 2]

   A is _____% of the total.

5. Draw a tape diagram to show the situation.

a) The number of girls is 25% of the total number of children.

   g:

   b:

b) The number of boys is 25% of the number of girls.

   g:

   b:

c) The number of girls is 80% of the number of boys.

   g:

   b:

d) The number of girls is 80% of the total number of children.

   g:

   b:

e) The number of boys is 75% of the total number of children.

   g:

   b:

f) The number of boys is 125% of the number of girls.

   g:

   b:

6. Which parts of Question 5 have the same tape diagram?

   Parts a) and _____, b) and _____, c) and _____.

7. Draw a tape diagram. Then complete the chart.

		Tape Diagram	Girls	Boys	Total
a)	The number of girls is 80% of the number of boys.	g: b:		30	
b)	The number of boys is 80% of the total number of children.	g: b:	20		
c)	The number of boys is 75% of the number of girls.	g: b:			35
d)	The number of boys is 75% of the total number of children.	g: b:	15		
e)	The number of girls is 120% of the number of boys.	g: b:		40	

8. Use a tape diagram to solve the problem.

a) The number of girls in a classroom is 60% of the number of boys. There are 12 girls in the classroom. How many students are in the class altogether?

b) The number of "yes" votes is 80% of the number of "no" votes. There were 45 votes altogether. How many were "yes" votes?

c) The number of fiction books in a library is 150% of the number of non-fiction books. The library has 4,000 books in total. How many fiction books and how many non-fiction books are in the library?

d) Students in a class read a book and watched the movie based on the book. 30% of the students preferred the book and the rest preferred the movie. If 21 people preferred the movie, how many people preferred the book?

Bonus ▶ The number of girls is 40% of the number of boys.

So the number of boys is _____% of the number of girls.

45. Percent More Than

1. What percent of B is the extra part of A?

a) A: [□□□□□□□]
   B: [□□□□] extra part of A

   The extra part of A is _____% of B.

b) A: [□□□]
   B: [□□]

   The extra part of A is _____% of B.

c) A: [□□□□]
   B: [□]

   The extra part of A is _____% of B.

d) A: [□□□□]
   B: [□□]

   The extra part of A is _____% of B.

e) A: [□□□□□]
   B: [□□□]

   The extra part of A is _____% of B.

f) A: [□□□□□□]
   B: [□□□□□]

   The extra part of A is _____% of B.

g) A: [□□□]
   B: [□]

   The extra part of A is _____% of B.

h) A: [□□□□□□□]
   B: [□□□□□]

   The extra part of A is _____% of B.

2. Draw a tape diagram so that the extra part of A is …

a) 20% of B

   A:

   B:

b) 25% of B

   A:

   B:

c) 60% of B

   A:

   B:

d) 150% of B

   A:

   B:

e) 120% of B

   A:

   B:

"There are 25% more girls than boys in a school" means that the number of "extra" girls is 25% of the number of boys.

Girls: ▢▢▢▢▢

Boys: ▢▢▢▢

The number of "extra" girls is the same as 25% of the boys.

3. Fill in the blanks.

a) g: ▢▢▢

b: ▢▢

The number of extra girls is what percent of the number of boys?

There are _____% more girls than boys.

b) g: ▢▢▢▢

b: ▢▢▢▢▢

The number of extra boys is what percent of the number of girls?

There are _____% more boys than girls.

c) g: ▢▢▢▢▢▢▢▢

b: ▢▢▢▢▢

There are _____% more girls than boys.

d) g: ▢▢

b: ▢▢▢▢▢

There are _____% more _____ than _____.

4. Draw a tape diagram to show the situation.

a) There are 50% more boys than girls.   b) There are 20% more girls than boys.

Bonus ▶ There are 120% more boys than girls.

5. Draw a tape diagram to answer the question.

a) There are 25% more boys than girls in a class. There are 36 students in the class altogether. How many boys and how many girls are in the class?

g: | 4 | 4 | 4 | 4 |

b: | 4 | 4 | 4 | 4 | 4 |

} 36 altogether

_____ boys and _____ girls

b) There are 50% more boys than girls in a class. There are 18 boys in the class. How many students are in the class altogether?

g:

b:

_____ students altogether

c) There are 20% more girls than boys in a class. There are 30 girls in the class. How many boys are in the class?

g:

b:

_____ boys

6. There are 25% more girls than boys in the school.

a) Draw a tape diagram to show the situation.

b) Use your tape diagram from part a) to complete the chart.

Number of Girls	Number of Boys	Total Number of Students
	360	
360		
		360

46. Ratios, Fractions, and Percentage Problems

1. Fill in the missing numbers for each classroom.

	Ratio of ...				What Fraction ...	
	girls to students	boys to students	girls to boys	boys to girls	are girls?	are boys?
a)	2 : 5	3 : 5	2 : 3	3 : 2	$\frac{2}{5}$	$\frac{3}{5}$
b)	5 : 7					
c)						$\frac{3}{4}$
d)		31 : 50				
e)				8 : 17		
f)						$\frac{1}{2}$
g)			7 : 11			
h)					$\frac{8}{15}$	
i)				31 : 25		

2. Fill in the missing numbers for each classroom.

	Percent That Are Girls	Percent That Are Boys	Fraction That Are Girls	Fraction That Are Boys	Ratio of Girls to Boys
a)	40%	60%	$\frac{40}{100}$	$\frac{60}{100}$	40 : 60
b)		45%			
c)				$\frac{1}{4}$	
d)					11 : 14
e)			$\frac{1}{2}$		
f)	85%				
g)					21 : 29

3. Show your answer with a tape diagram.

a) $\frac{3}{5}$ of the students are girls.

The ratio of boys to girls is _____ to _____.

There are _____% more girls than boys.

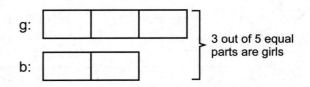

g:

b:

3 out of 5 equal parts are girls

b) $\frac{4}{9}$ of the students are girls.

The ratio of boys to girls is _____ to _____.

There are _____% more boys than girls.

c) $\frac{6}{11}$ of the students are boys.

The ratio of boys to girls is _____ to _____.

There are _____% more _____

than _____.

d) $\frac{1}{3}$ of the students are girls.

The ratio of boys to girls is _____ to _____.

There are _____% more _____

than _____.

e) $\frac{7}{12}$ of the students are boys.

The ratio of boys to girls is _____ to _____.

There are _____% more _____

than _____.

f) $\frac{5}{14}$ of the students are boys.

The ratio of boys to girls is _____ to _____.

There are _____% more _____

than _____.

4. Draw a tape diagram, then complete the chart.

		Tape Diagram	Girls	Boys	Total
a)	The number of girls is 80% more than the number of boys.	g: b:		30	
b)	The fraction of students that are girls is $\frac{5}{9}$.	g: b:	20		
c)	The number of boys is 40% of the number of girls.	g: b:			35
d)	The ratio of girls to boys is 5 : 8.	g: b:	15		

5. Show your answer with a tape diagram.

a) There are 20% more boys than girls in a class.

The ratio of boys to girls is _____ to _____.

b) The ratio of girls to boys in a class is 5 : 4. There are _____% more girls than boys.

c) $\frac{3}{5}$ of the students in a class are girls. There are _____% more girls than boys.

6. a) There are 10% more boys than girls in Grade 7. There are 5 more boys than girls. How many boys and how many girls are in Grade 7?

b) The ratio of boys to girls in Grade 7 is 11 : 10. There are 5 more boys than girls. How many boys and how many girls are in Grade 7?

c) Why should your answers to parts a) and b) be the same?

47. Scale Drawings and Similar Shapes

1. a) Draw a triangle that has the same shape, but is twice as long and twice as tall.

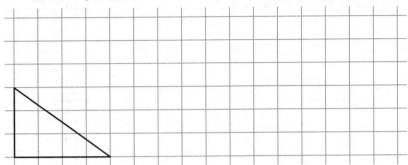

b) Measure the third side of each triangle. Is the third side twice as long, too? _____

When you make a new drawing by multiplying every side by the same number, the drawing is called a **scale drawing**.

2. Here are three scale drawings.

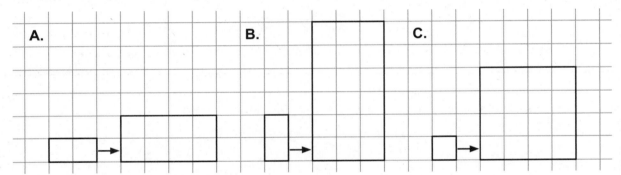

a) What is the ratio (original length) : (new length)? Hint: The length is the longest side.

   A. _____   **B.** _____   **C.** _____

b) What is the ratio (original width) : (new width)? Hint: The width is the shortest side.

   A. _____   **B.** _____   **C.** _____

c) Are the ratios from part a) and part b) equivalent? If not, find your mistake.

3. Finish the scale drawing.

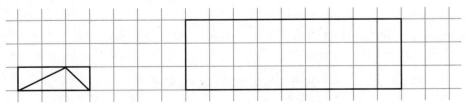

Two shapes are **similar** if they are the same shape, but have different sizes. You can make a similar shape by making a scale drawing.

4. Find the missing side lengths in the similar rectangles. Include the units.

a)
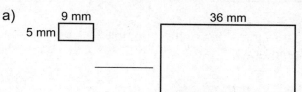

b)
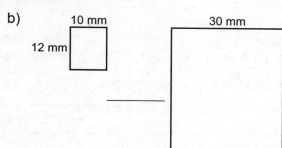

c)
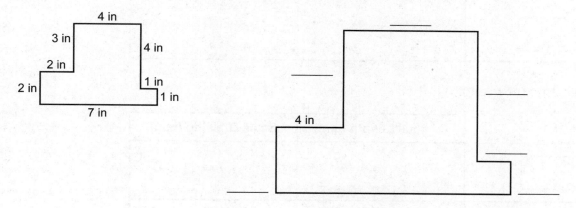

5. The two shapes are similar. Find the missing side lengths. Include the units.

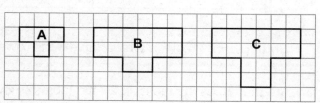

6. Which of these shapes are similar? How do you know?

_____

_____

_____

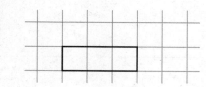

7. On grid paper, draw another rectangle by increasing both the length and the width by 1 unit. Is your drawing a scale drawing of the original shape?

48. Scale Drawings and Ratio Tables

1. Bold the line in the scale drawing that matches the bold line in the original drawing.

a)    b)    c)

2. Jane wants to draw a scale drawing of the shape. Measure the sides of the original shape, then write the lengths of the new lines Jane should draw.

a) (original length) : (new length) = 1 : 2

	Original Length (mm)	Scale Drawing (mm)
	15	30

b) (original length) : (new length) = 1 : 3

	Original Length (mm)	Scale Drawing (mm)

REMINDER: A table is a ratio table if the rows are equivalent ratios.

3. Are the tables in Question 2 ratio tables? How do you know? Hint: What unit ratio is each row equivalent to?

_____

_____

_____

The **length** of a rectangle is the length of its longer side.

The **width** of a rectangle is the length of its shorter side.

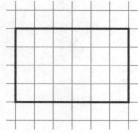

length ← → width

4. a) The table shows the measurements of a rectangular field. Complete the ratio table, then draw the field to the scale indicated.

i)

	Actual (m)	Scale Drawing (grid squares)
Scale	15	2
Length	45	6
Width	30	4

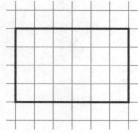

ii)

	Actual (m)	Scale Drawing (grid squares)
Scale	6	1
Length	30	
Width	12	

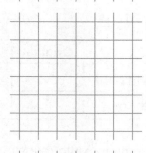

iii)

	Actual (m)	Scale Drawing (grid squares)
Scale	5	2
Length	15	
Width	5	

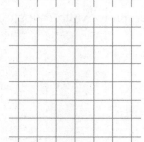

b) Find the "length : width" ratios from part a).

	i)	ii)	iii)
Length to Width Ratio (actual)	45 : 30		
Length to Width Ratio (scale)	6 : 4		

c) Write the ratios from part b) using the smallest whole numbers you can.

	i)	ii)	iii)
Length to Width Ratio (actual)	3 : 2		
Length to Width Ratio (scale)	3 : 2		

d) Are the length to width ratios equivalent in the actual and scale drawings?

i) _____   ii) _____   iii) _____

The unit ratio (original length) : (new length) = 1 : ? tells you what number to multiply the original length by to get the new length. The unit ratio can be a fraction.

Remember: You can multiply a fraction by a whole number.

$$\frac{3}{4} \times 12 = \frac{3}{4} \text{ of } 12$$
$$= 3 \times \left(\frac{1}{4} \text{ of } 12 \right)$$
$$= 3 \times (12 \div 4)$$
$$= 3 \times 3 = 9$$

5. a) Write the ratio (original length) : (new length) as a unit ratio, then complete the ratio table.

   i) 4 : 3 = 1 : _____

	Original	Scale
Length (cm)	12	
Width (cm)	8	

   ii) 5 : 2 = 1 : _____

	Original	Scale
Length (cm)	20	
Width (cm)	15	

   b) Are the length to width ratios equivalent in the original and scale drawings?

   i)   ii)

   _____   _____

When two rectangles are similar, the length : width ratio is the same in both drawings.

6. Find the missing length two ways. Make sure you get the same answer both ways.

   Original   Scale
        5   4

   2 [ ] → ? [ ]

   a) Make "length : width" ratios the same in both drawings.

Length	Width

   b) Make "original : scale" ratios the same for both the length and the width.

Original	Scale

49. Scale Drawings in the Real World

1. On the map, the scale is 1 mm : 50 mi. Use the scale to determine the distances in real life.

Chicago ●

● New York City

Los Angeles ●

● Houston

		Distance on Map (mm)	Distance in Real Life (mi)
a)	From Chicago to Houston		
b)	From Chicago to New York City		
c)	From Chicago to Los Angeles		
d)	From New York City to Houston		
e)	From New York City to Los Angeles		
f)	From Los Angeles to Houston		

2. On the floor plan, the scale is 1 grid square : 20 in. Use the scale to determine the lengths in real life. Include the units in your answers.

		On Floor Plan	In Real Life
a)	How long is the closet?		
b)	How long is the bed?		
c)	What are the dimensions of the washroom?		
d)	How far from the TV is the couch?		
e)	How wide is the table?		

f) The kitchen countertop, which includes the stove, fridge, microwave, and sink along one wall, is shown in gray. If the stove is 30 inches wide, the fridge 28 inches wide, the microwave 24 inches wide, and the sink 32 inches wide, how much countertop space is left?

3. A room is 15 ft wide and 20 ft long. Draw the room to the given scale.

    a) 1 grid square : 5 ft   b) 2 grid squares : 5 ft

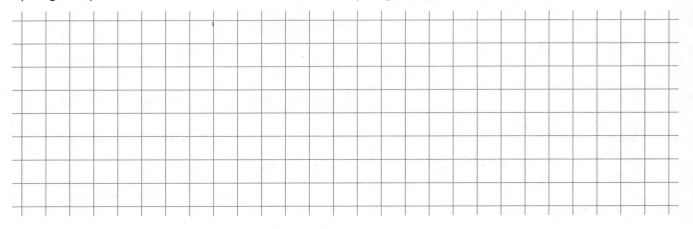

    c) 3 grid squares : 5 ft

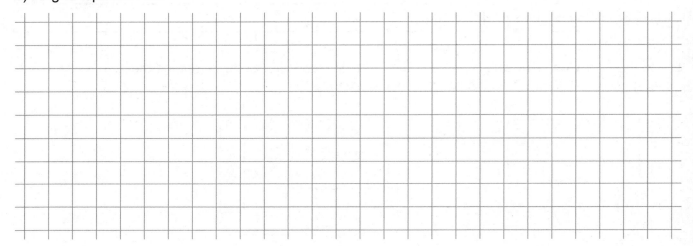

4. A closet is 4 ft wide and 6 ft long. Draw the closet to the given scale.

    a) 1 grid square : 2 ft   b) 3 grid squares : 2 ft

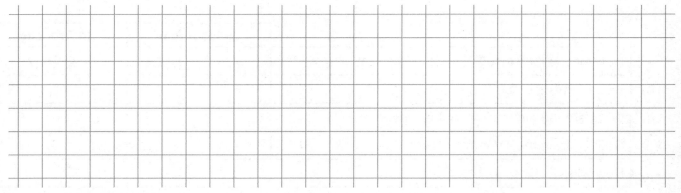

Bonus ▶ A is a scale drawing of B with (original length) : (scaled length) = 1 : 2.

            B is a scale drawing of C with (original length) : (scaled length) = 1 : 3.

            A is a scale drawing of C with (original length) : (scaled length) = 1 : _____.

5. The scale drawing of a room has the scale 1 grid square : 3 ft.

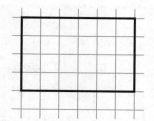

   a) How long is the room? _____

   b) How wide is the room? _____

   c) Draw the same room to the given scale.

   i)   1 grid square : 6 ft   ii) 1 grid square : 2 ft

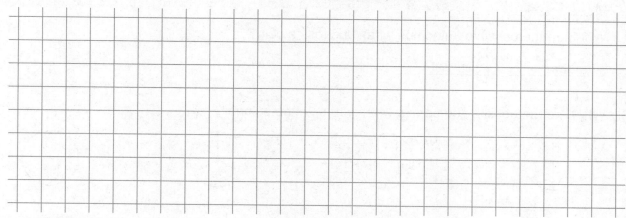

   iii) 2 grid squares : 3 ft   **Bonus ▶** 1 grid square : 4 ft

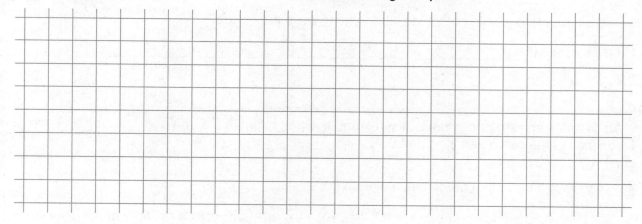

6. The map is drawn using a scale of 3 grid squares to 2 mi.
Draw another map using the scale 1 in to 4 mi.
Hint: Rewrite the scale as _____ in : 1 mi.

7. A window is drawn to the scale
(scale length) : (actual length) = 2 cm : 1 ft.
The drawing is 6 cm high and 10 cm wide.
Draw another picture of the window with scale 1 cm : 2 ft.

Dragon Lair

8. The killer whale is drawn to the scale 1 cm = 6 ft.
How long is the actual whale?

50. Events and Outcomes

Any time you do something that has different possible results, you are doing an **experiment**.

Example: If Rick rolls a die, there are 6 possible results. He could roll a 1, 2, 3, 4, 5, or 6.

The different results of an experiment are called **outcomes**.

1. What are the possible outcomes when you toss a coin?

   ___heads___ , _____

2. What are the possible outcomes when you spin the spinner?

   a)
   b)
   c)
   d)

   ___1, 2, 3, 4___   _____   _____   _____

3. What are the possible outcomes when you throw a paper cup?

   It could land _____ , or _____ ,

   or _____ .

An **event** is any set of outcomes. For example, when rolling a die, the event "rolling an even number" consists of the outcomes 2, 4, and 6.

4. Lynn rolls a die. What outcomes make up the event?

   a) Lynn rolls an odd number: _____   b) Lynn rolls a multiple of 3: _____

   c) Lynn rolls a multiple of 5: _____   d) Lynn rolls a prime number: _____

   e) Lynn rolls a number greater than 4: _____

   f) Lynn rolls a number less than 3: _____

5. Shade the outcomes from spinning the spinner that make up the event.

   a) red (R)

   b) blue (B)

   c) 7

   d) a multiple of 3

6. How many outcomes make up the event of spinning ...

    a) the letter N _____

    b) the letter W _____

    c) the letter C _____

    d) a letter in "NEW YORK" _____

An event is **impossible** if there are no outcomes that produce it.

Example: Rolling a 7 on a regular die is impossible because there is no side with 7 dots.

An event is **certain** if all possible outcomes produce it.

Example: Rolling a number less than 10 on a regular die is certain because all sides are numbered with less than 10 dots.

Any other event is **in between** certain and impossible.

7. The spinner can spin red (R) or blue (B). Is the event certain, impossible, or in between?

    a) Spinning red is _____ .

    b) Spinning green is _____ .

    c) Spinning blue is _____ .

    d) Spinning a color used to make purple is _____ .

8. Should the spinner land more often on white or gray?

    a)   b)   c)   d)

    _____   _____   _____   _____

An outcome or event is **more likely** than another if it should happen more often.

9. Write "more likely than," "as likely as," or "less likely than." Spinning green (G) is ...

    a) _____ spinning blue (B).

    b) _____ spinning red (R).

    c) _____ spinning yellow (Y).

    d) _____ spinning orange (O).

    Bonus ▶ Which is more likely: spinning a primary color (R, B, Y) or a secondary color (G, P, O)?

    _____

You can use a **probability line** to show how likely an event is. An event has an **even** chance of happening if it happens half the time.

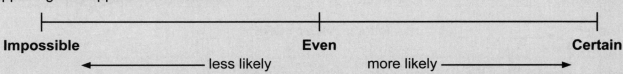

Impossible   ← less likely   Even   more likely →   Certain

10. Mark a point on the line to show how likely each event is.

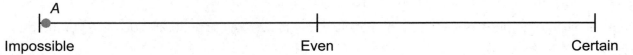

Impossible   Even   Certain

A. It will snow in New York City in August.

B. You roll a 6 on a regular die.

C. You will see a stranger today.

D. You will see a wolf today.

E. You get heads when tossing a coin.

F. You roll an 8 on a regular die.

G. The sun will set in the East.

H. The sun will set in the West.

When all the outcomes are equally likely, you can compare how likely two events are by counting their outcomes.

Example: On the spinner, spinning red (3 outcomes) is more likely than spinning blue (2 outcomes) because 3 is more than 2.

---

11. a) List all of the outcomes that are …

    i)   even numbers _____

    ii)   odd numbers _____

    iii)   greater than 5 _____

    iv)   a factor of 5 _____

   b) Which event is more likely?

    i)   an odd number or an even number _____

    ii)   a number greater than 5 or a factor of 5 _____

12. Carlos says that spinning red is more likely than spinning blue because two outcomes are red and only one outcome is blue. Is he correct? Explain how you know.

Bonus ▶ Can you create a spinner where spinning a number greater than 3 is less likely than spinning a number greater than 5? Explain.

51. Probability

The probability of an **impossible event** is **0**. The probability of a **certain event** is **1**. The probability of any event is a number between 0 and 1.

Example: When tossing a coin, getting heads is 1 out of 2 equally likely outcomes. So the probability of getting heads is $\frac{1}{2}$.

1. Fill in the blanks. What is the probability of spinning red?

a) B | G / R _____ out of
_____ outcomes is red.

The probability of spinning red is _____.

b) B | R / Y | G _____ out of
_____ outcomes is red.

The probability of spinning red is _____.

c) R | G / R _____ out of
_____ outcomes are red.

The probability of spinning red is _____.

d) R | B / B | R / R _____ out of
_____ outcomes are red.

The probability of spinning red is _____.

When all outcomes are equally likely, the probability of an event is:

$$\frac{\text{\# of outcomes when the event happens}}{\text{\# of outcomes in total}}$$

2. a) What is the probability of spinning the color?

  i) red _____   ii) blue _____   iii) green _____

b) Show the probability of each event on the probability line.

A. Spinning red   **B.** Spinning blue   **C.** Spinning green

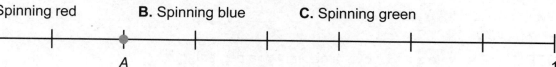

3. Hanna plays on a basketball team. Write each probability as a fraction.

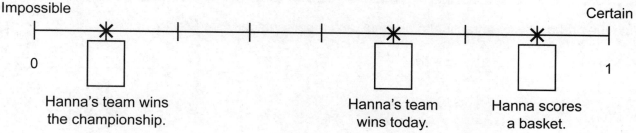

Impossible   Certain

0   1

Hanna's team wins the championship.   Hanna's team wins today.   Hanna scores a basket.

4. The six outcomes from rolling a regular die are: 1, 2, 3, 4, 5, or 6.
   Complete the table. Write the probability as a fraction in lowest terms.

	Event	Outcomes When the Event Happens	Probability of Event
a)	Rolling an even number.	2, 4, 6	$\frac{3}{6} = \frac{1}{2}$
b)	Rolling a number greater than 4.		
c)	Rolling an odd number.		
d)	Rolling a prime number.		
e)	Rolling a multiple of 5.		
f)	Rolling a factor of 12.		

5. When Zack spins the spinner, he says the probability of spinning red is $\frac{1}{3}$ because it is 1 out of 3 possible outcomes. Explain his mistake.

6. A class has 12 boys and 13 girls. A student is chosen to make the morning announcements.

   a) How many students are in the class? _____

   b) What is the probability the student is a girl? _____

   c) What percent of the students are girls? _____

   d) Are your answers to b) and c) equivalent? _____

> REMINDER: You can write a fraction as a decimal or a percentage.
>
> Examples: $\frac{3}{10} = 0.3 = 30\%$ $\frac{4}{5} = \frac{8}{10} = 0.8 = 80\%$ $\frac{3}{4} = \frac{75}{100} = 0.75 = 75\%$

7. Write the probability as a fraction, a decimal, and a percentage.

   a) P(R) = $\frac{2}{5}$ = __0.4__ = __40%__   b) P(B) = ___ = _____ = _____

   c) P(G) = ___ = _____ = _____

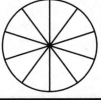

8. Write the letters A, B, and C on the spinner so that the probability of spinning
   an A is 0.3, a B is 0.5, and a C is 0.2.

9. The probability of rain is often given as a percentage. Write a fraction for the prediction. Reduce your answer to lowest terms.

   a) 60% chance of rain   b) 35% chance of rain   c) 75% chance of rain

   _____   _____   _____

10. Describe an event that has the given probability of occurring.

    a) 100% _____

    b) 50% _____

    c) 0% _____

In baseball, a **batting average** is the ratio of the number of hits to the number of times a player has a turn at bat. Batting averages are decimals that can be changed to fractions out of 1,000.

Example: A batting average of .427 ($= \frac{427}{1,000}$) means a player had 427 hits in 1,000 times at bat.

11. Find the probability of a hit given a player's batting average. Write your answer as a fraction in lowest terms.

   a) .125   b) .300   c) .475   d) .256   e) .324

12. Which player is most likely to have a hit?

   a) Player A: batting average .425   b) Player A: hits one quarter of pitches
      Player B: hits 4 out of 10 pitches   Player B: batting average .230
      Player C: hits 42% of pitches   Player C: hits 23% of pitches

13. Write numbers on the spinner to match the probability. The probability of spinning ...

   a) a 3 is 50%   b) a 2 is $\frac{1}{3}$ c) a 3 is 0.4   d) an even number is $\frac{5}{6}$

14. Draw lines to cut the spinner into equal parts. Write the probability of the given event.

   a)   b)   c)   d)

   P(B) = _____   P(R) = _____   P(Y) = _____   P(G) = _____

52. Expectation

Sharon plans to spin the spinner 15 times to see how many times it will land on yellow.

Since $\frac{1}{3}$ of the spinner is yellow, Sharon expects to land on yellow $\frac{1}{3}$ of the time.

Sharon finds $\frac{1}{3}$ of 15 by dividing: $15 \div 3 = 5$.

So she expects the spinner to land on yellow 5 times.

1. If you flip a coin repeatedly, what fraction of the throws would you expect to be heads? _____

2. How many times would you expect to flip heads if you flipped a coin …

   a) 12 times? _____   b) 40 times? _____   c) 68 times? _____

3. a) Divide.

   i) $96 \div 2 =$ _____   ii) $96 \div 3 =$ _____   iii) $96 \div 4 =$ _____   iv) $96 \div 6 =$ _____

   b) To do the division in part a), did you …

   A. divide mentally?   **B.** use a calculator?   **C.** use long division?

   i) _____   ii) _____   iii) _____   iv) _____

   c) How many times would you expect the spinner to land on red after 96 spins?

   i)   ii)   iii)   iv)

   _____   _____   _____   _____

4. How many times would you expect to land on yellow if you spin the spinner …

   a)   18 times? _____
   69 times? _____

   b)   24 times? _____
   92 times? _____

   c)   15 times? _____
   40 times? _____

   d)   8 times? _____
   80 times? _____

   e)   12 times? _____
   30 times? _____

   f)   12 times? _____
   30 times? _____

5. Place the point of your pencil inside a paper clip in the middle of the spinner. Be sure to hold the pencil still so you can spin the paper clip around the pencil.

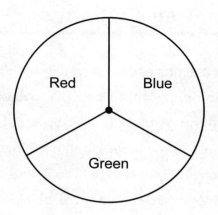

a) If you spin the spinner 30 times, how many times would you predict spinning red?

b) Spin the spinner 30 times. Make a tally of your results. Were your results exactly the same as your expectations? Were they close?

6. If you spin the spinner 18 times …

a) how many of your spins would you expect to be green? _____

b) which of the charts shows a result you would be most likely to get? _____

A	
Green	Red
̵HHt ̵||	̵HHt ̵HHt ̵|

B	
Green	Red
̵HHt ̵HHt	̵HHt ̵|||

C	
Green	Red
̵HHt ̵HHt ̵HHt ̵||	̵|

c) which result would surprise you? _____

REMINDER: Since $\frac{1}{3}$ of 15 is 5, we know that $\frac{2}{3}$ of 15 is $2 \times 5 = 10$.

---

7. How many times do you expect each spinner to land on red if you spin each 300 times?

a)   _____ and   _____

b)   _____ and 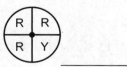 _____

8. How many times would you expect the spinner to land on red in 300 spins? Explain how you found your answer.

53. Tree Diagrams

At a sports camp, David can choose from the following activities:

Morning: gymnastics (G) or canoeing (C)

Afternoon: hockey (H), soccer (S), or rugby (R)

David draws a tree diagram so that he can see all of the combinations of options.

Step 1: He writes his two morning options at the ends of two branches.

Step 2: Under each of his morning options, he adds three branches—one for each of his afternoon options.

Step 3: Follow any path along the branches (from the top of the tree to the bottom) to find one of David's options.

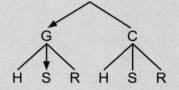

The path highlighted by the arrows shows gymnastics in the morning and soccer in the afternoon.

1. Follow a path from the top of the tree to a box at the bottom, and write the sports named on the path in the box. Continue until you have filled in all the boxes.

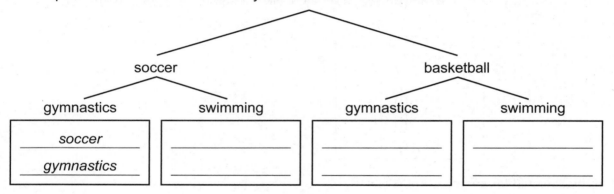

2. Complete the tree diagram to show all of the possible outcomes of flipping a coin twice (H = heads and T = tails).

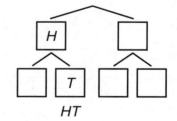

3. Marla's camp offers the following activities:

Morning: drama (D) or art (A)

Afternoon: poetry (P) or fiction (F)

Draw a tree diagram (like the one in Question 1) to show all the combinations of options.

4. Complete the tree diagram to show all of the possible outcomes of flipping the coin then spinning the spinner.

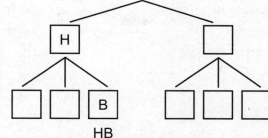

HB

5. a) Complete the tree diagram to show all the outcomes when you toss a coin then roll a die.

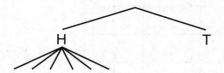

b) Complete the tree diagram to show all the outcomes when you roll a die then toss a coin.

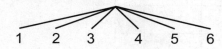

1　2　3　4　5　6

6. A restaurant offers the following options for breakfast:

Main Course: eggs (E), muffins (M), or pancakes (P)

Juice: apple (A), tomato (T), orange (O), or grape (G)

Draw a tree diagram to show all the different breakfasts you could order.

7. a) Use the tree diagrams you drew for Questions 4, 5, and 6 to fill in the chart.

Question	Number of Branches at the First Level	Number of Branches at the Second Level	Total Number of Paths
4	2	3	6
5.a)			
5.b)			
6			

b) How can you calculate the total number of paths from the number of branches at each level? Explain.

54. Charts and Organized Lists

1. Ross flips a coin twice. Shade the given event. Then find the probability.

a) two heads

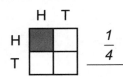

$\dfrac{1}{4}$

b) two tails

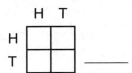

_____

c) one head and one tail

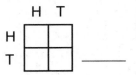

_____

2. Micky rolls two dice. Shade the given event. Write the probability as a fraction in lowest terms.

a) rolls a sum of 7

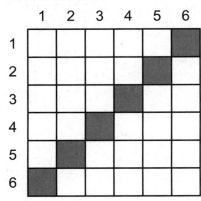

$\dfrac{6}{36} = \dfrac{1}{6}$

b) rolls a sum of 4

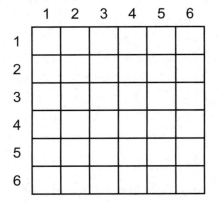

_____

c) rolls a 3 and a 4

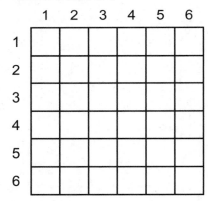

_____

d) rolls double 6s

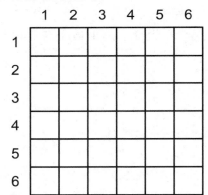

_____

e) both dice show the same number

f) rolls at least one 3

g) rolls an even total

h) the numbers are 1 apart

3. a) If you roll two dice, how many outcomes are there? _____

b) If you roll a die twice, how many outcomes are there? _____

c) Are your answers to parts a) and b) the same? Why does this make sense?

Will wants to make an **organized list** of all the outcomes from spinning Spinner A and then Spinner B.

Step 1: There are **3 outcomes** on Spinner B, so Will lists each outcome on Spinner A **3 times**:

1   1   1   2   2   2

Spinner A   **Spinner B**

Step 2: Beside each outcome from Spinner A, Will writes the 3 outcomes from Spinner B:

1R   1Y   1B   2R   2Y   2B

The list shows there are **6 outcomes** altogether.

4. Blanca tosses a coin then rolls a die. Finish making an organized list to show all the outcomes.

H1   H2   H3   _____   _____   _____   _____   _____   _____   _____   _____

5. Sal tosses a coin then spins the spinner.

a) Make an organized list to show all the outcomes.

i)

<u>H1 H2 T1 T2</u> _____

ii)

_____

iii)

_____

iv)

_____

b) How many outcomes does each event from part a) have?

i) _____   ii) _____   iii) _____   iv) _____

A game is **fair** if the chance of winning equals the chance of losing.

6. Randi rolls a die then spins the spinner.

a) Make an organized list to show all the possible outcomes.

b) Greg plays a game where he wins and loses as follows:

He wins if he rolls an even number then spins yellow.
He loses if he rolls a multiple of 3 then spins red.

Find the probability of winning and losing. Is the game fair?

7. Anne's camp offers the following activities:

Morning: swimming (S), or tennis (T)

Afternoon: canoeing (C), baseball (B), or hiking (H)

Anne needs to bring her running shoes if she chooses tennis, baseball, or hiking.
She needs to bring a towel if she chooses swimming or canoeing.

Circle the outcomes that show the event.

a) Anne needs her running shoes.

    SC   SB   SH   TC   TB   TH

b) Anne needs a towel.

    SC   SB   SH   TC   TB   TH

c) Anne needs her running shoes and a towel.

    SC   SB   SH   TC   TB   TH

d) Anne needs her running shoes for the morning and the afternoon.

    SC   SB   SH   TC   TB   TH

8. If the activities are chosen randomly, find the probability of each event in Question 7.

a) _____   b) _____   c) _____   d) _____

A contest between two people is **fair** if they both have the same chance of winning.

---

9. a) Make an organized list of all the possible outcomes of spinning both spinners.

   b) Find the probability that the outcomes from the two spinners ...

     i) add to 6   ii) multiply to 6   iii) add to 4

     _____   _____   _____

   c) Ed and Beth play a game in which they each spin one of the spinners. Ed wins if the results add to 6. Beth wins if the results multiply to 6. Is the game fair? If not, who has the better chance of winning?

   d) Make up a fair game for Ed and Beth to play using the spinners.

10. A tetrahedral die has 4 vertices numbered from 1 to 4. When you roll this die, there is always a vertex on top. Make a chart to show all the combinations for rolling a pair of tetrahedral dice.

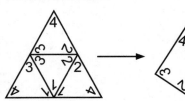 This is a "4" vertex.
There is a 4 hidden on the back face.

55. More Tree Diagrams, Charts, and Organized Lists

1. Bo plays a game with two spinners. Draw a chart to show all the outcomes. Then fill
   in the blanks.

   a) Spinner 1 has __2__ outcomes.

      Spinner 2 has __3__ outcomes.

      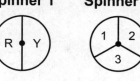
      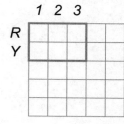

      Spinning both spinners has __6__ outcomes.

   b) Spinner 1 has _____ outcomes.

      Spinner 2 has _____ outcomes.

      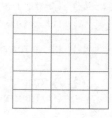

      Spinning both spinners has _____ outcomes.

   c) Spinner 1 has _____ outcomes.

      Spinner 2 has _____ outcomes.

      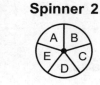
      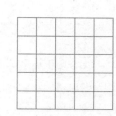

      Spinning both spinners has _____ outcomes.

2. Make an organized list to show that there are 2 groups of 5 outcomes
   when spinning the two spinners.

3. a) How can you find the number of outcomes for spinning both spinners from the
      number of outcomes for spinning each spinner?

      _____

   b) If Spinner 1 has 100 outcomes and Spinner 2 has 50 outcomes, how many outcomes
      would there be for spinning both spinners?

      _____

4. Jenny rolls a die with 20 faces, then a die with 12 faces. How many possible outcomes
   are there?

5. Make an organized list of all the outcomes.

a)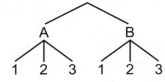

b)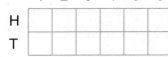

	1	2	3	4	5	6
H						
T						

6. In a role-playing game, Jay's character is exploring a tunnel in a cave.

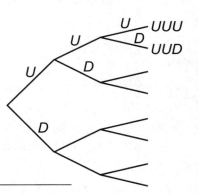

a) Complete the tree diagram that shows all the paths through the cave. (U = up, D = down)

b) How many paths are there through the cave? _____

c) A monster is waiting at the end of one path. Do you think it is likely or unlikely that Jay's character will meet the monster? Explain.

_____

_____

7. Tess has two sets of paints:

Set 1: red, blue, and yellow   **Set 2:** red and blue

She chooses one color from each set at random and mixes them.

a) Make a chart, a tree diagram, and an organized list to show all the possible outcomes.

b) Find the probability that Tess makes ...

   i) green   ii) blue   iii) yellow   iv) purple

c) Did you use the chart, the tree diagram, or the organized list from part a) to do part b)?

8. Find the probability by making a tree diagram or a chart. Explain your choice.

a) Rolling two dice results in at least one 3.

b) Tossing four coins results in at least 3 heads.

9. Cereal boxes come with a picture of either a cat or a dog inside. There are the same number of boxes with each picture. You win a prize if you collect one of each picture.

a) Use a tree diagram to find the probability that you will win a prize if you buy ...

   i) 2 boxes   ii) 3 boxes   iii) 4 boxes

b) Does the probability of winning a prize increase with the number of boxes you buy? Did you expect this?

JUMP Math Accumula

56. Empirical Probability

REMINDER: Two quantities are proportional if the T-table comparing their values is a ratio table (i.e., the rows are equivalent ratios).

1. a) Complete the chart.

i)

Spins	Expected Red
30	
60	
150	

ii)

Spins	Expected Red
40	
120	
240	

iii)

Spins	Expected Even Numbers
5	
50	
200	

iv)

Spins	Expected Prime Numbers
10	
40	
65	

b) Are the tables in part a) ratio tables?

i) _____   ii) _____   iii) _____   iv) _____

If you don't know what a spinner looks like, you can use what actually happens to estimate it.

Example: A spinner lands on red 17 times in 20 spins. How many times would you expect it to land on red in 100 spins?

You can use equivalent ratios to find out:

$$\times 5 \left(\begin{array}{c} 17 : 20 \\ ? : 100 \end{array} \right) \times 5$$

You would expect the spinner to land on red 85 times in 100 spins.

2. Billy randomly picked 100 of the 800 students at his school and asked them how they get to school. 12 of them said they bike. How many students at his school should he expect to bike to school?

3. A bag contained 10,000 red chips and white chips. Amy reached in and grabbed a chip. She looked at it, then put it back. She did this 40 times and got red 9 times. How many red chips do you estimate are in the bag?

4. A spinner landed on red 12 times in 50 spins. How many times would you expect it to land on red in 1,000 spins?

5. A baseball player had 24 hits in 96 times at bat. How many hits would you expect the player to get in 1,000 times at bat?

The **theoretical probability** is what should happen. The **empirical probability** is what does happen.

$$\text{Empirical probability of A} = \frac{\text{\# of times A happened}}{\text{\# of experiments performed}}$$

When you don't know the theoretical probability, you can estimate it by repeating an experiment many times and using the empirical probability.

6. Do the experiment 25 times. Record your results in the table. Ask three other people for their results. Complete the table. Make sure your "Total" row adds to 100.

a) Toss a coin.

	Heads	Tails
My results		
Partner 1		
Partner 2		
Partner 3		
Total		

b) Toss a paper cup.

Lands Upright	Lands Upside Down	Lands on Its Side

Use your answers to Question 6 to answer Questions 7, 8, and 9.

7. a) What is the theoretical probability of getting heads? _____

b) What is your total empirical probability of getting heads? _____

c) Ethan flipped a coin 5 times and got 4 heads. What is Ethan's empirical probability

of getting heads? _____

d) Whose empirical probability is closer to the theoretical probability, yours or Ethan's? Why does that make sense?

_____

8. Write "as likely as," "more likely than," or "less likely than."

a) A coin landing on heads appears to be _____ a coin landing on tails.

b) A paper cup landing upright appears to be _____ a paper cup landing upside down.

9. Estimate the probability that a paper cup will land …

a) upright _____   b) upside down _____   c) on its side _____

10. A bottle cap was tossed 1,000 times, with the following results:

Lands Flat Side Down	Lands Flat Side Up	Lands on Its Side
894	65	41

a) What is the empirical probability of the outcome? Write the answer as a fraction
   and a decimal.

   i)   lands flat side down   ii)   lands flat side up   iii) lands on its side

   _____   _____   _____

b) Place the probabilities approximately on the number line from 0 to 1.

   A. lands flat side up   **B.** lands flat side down   **C.** lands on its side

   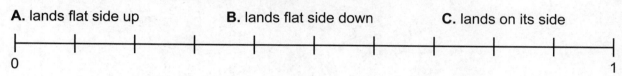

   0   1

c) What is the most likely outcome? _____

d) What is the least likely outcome? _____

e) If you tossed the bottle cap 10,000 times, how many times would you expect it to

   land on its side? _____

11. a) How many times would you expect the spinner to land on red if

   you spin it 15 times? _____

   b) Kathy spins the spinner 15 times and it lands on red 8 times.
   Explain why this doesn't contradict your result from part a).

   _____

   _____

   c) Kathy thinks that if she spins the spinner 1,500 times, it will land on red 800 times.
   Explain her mistake.

   _____

   _____

   _____

12. A school goes from Grades 1 to 5 and has 800 students in total. Jack asked the
25 students in a Grade 5 class how they get to school. Ten of them said they bike.

Jack predicted the number of students who bike to school would be $\frac{10}{25} \times 800 = \frac{2}{5} \times 800 = 320$.

In fact, only 135 students bike to school. What was his mistake? Hint: Are all students
equally likely to bike to school?

57. Solving Equations—Guess and Check

Remember: Finding the value of a variable that makes an equation true is called solving for the variable. Sara uses a table to solve $2x + 1 = 7$.

x	$2x + 1$	Is the equation true?
1	3	✗
2	5	✗
3	7	✓

So $x = 3$ makes the equation true.

1. Complete the table, then solve for x.

a) $4x + 1 = 21$

x	$4x + 1$	True?
1	$4(1) + 1 = 5$	✗
2	$4(2) + 1 = 9$	✗
3		
4		
5		

So $x = $ _____

b) $3x + 4 = 16$

x	$3x + 4$	True?
1	$3(1) + 4 = 7$	✗
2		
3		
4		
5		

So $x = $ _____

c) $5x - 3 = 12$

x	$5x - 3$	True?
1		
2		
3		
4		
5		

So $x = $ _____

2. Replace n with 5 and say whether 5 is too high, too low, or just right to solve the equation. Then try a lower or higher number if you need to.

a) $4n - 1 = 23$

n	$4n - 1$	Answer
5	$4(5) - 1$	19

5 is ___too low___.

b) $5n - 4 = 16$

n	$5n - 4$	Answer
5	$5(5) - 4$	

5 is _____.

c) $2n - 5 = 7$

n	$2n - 5$	Answer
5		

5 is _____.

d) $3n + 2 = 17$

n	$3n + 2$	Answer
5		

5 is _____.

e) $4n + 3 = 19$

n	$4n + 3$	Answer
5		

5 is _____.

f) $8n - 1 = 31$

n	$8n - 1$	Answer
5		

5 is _____.

3. Solve for n by guessing small values for n, checking, and revising.

a) $4n + 2 = 22$

b) $5n - 2 = 33$

c) $4n - 1 = 27$

d) $6n - 5 = 19$

e) $8n - 2 = 22$

f) $9n + 2 = 65$

4. Complete the table. When n increases, does the expression increase or decrease?

a)

n	$n - 2$
1	
2	
3	
4	

As n increases, $n - 2$

_____.

b)

n	$2 - n$
1	
2	
3	
4	

As n increases, $2 - n$

_____.

c)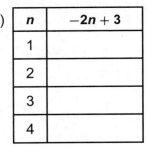

n	$-2n + 3$
1	
2	
3	
4	

As n increases, $-2n + 3$

_____.

> When the coefficient of n is negative, increasing n makes the expression smaller.
>
> You can use this to solve $15 - 2n = 7$ by guessing and checking. Guess $n = 5$ and evaluate:
>
> $15 - 2(5) = 15 - 10 = 5$
>
> The answer is too *low*, so 5 is too *high*. Try $n = 4$ in the expression:
>
> $15 - 2(4) = 15 - 8 = 7$
>
> So $n = 4$ solves the equation.

5. Replace n with 5 and say whether 5 is too high or too low to solve the equation.
Then try a lower or higher number.

a) $30 - 4n = 14$

n	$30 - 4n$	Answer
5		

5 is _____.

b) $50 - 5n = 20$

n	$50 - 5n$	Answer
5		

5 is _____.

c) $22 - 3n = 4$

n	$22 - 3n$	Answer
5		

5 is _____.

6. Solve for n by guessing small values for n, checking, and revising.

a) $20 - 3n = 8$

b) $5n - 4 = 26$

c) $50 - 7n = 15$

d) $32 - 6n = -4$

e) $9n - 34 = 2$

f) $6n - 25 = 5$

7. Would you solve $\dfrac{7}{3} - \dfrac{1}{8}x = \dfrac{2}{5}$ by guessing, checking, and revising? Explain.

58. Preserving Equality to Solve Equations

1. Show the operation you need to do to get back to x.

a) $3x$

$\underline{\quad 3x \div 3 \quad}$

b) $x - 3$

c) $x + 7$

d) $8 + x$

e) $\dfrac{x}{8}$

f) $1.5x$

g) $x - 9$

h) $x + \dfrac{3}{4}$

To solve an equation, put the variable by itself on one side of the equation, with coefficient 1.

Example: $x - 3 = 4$ Adding 3 gets $x - 3$ back to x, so add 3 to both sides of the equation.

$x - 3 + 3 = 4 + 3$ Since both sides are equal before adding 3, they are equal after adding 3.

$x = 7$ Now x is by itself, with coefficient 1, so you can read the answer: $x = 7$.

---

2. Get back to x on the left side. Do the same operation to the right side to solve the equation.

a) $x - 3 = 5$

$x - 3 + 3 = 5 + 3$

$x = 8$

b) $x + 8 = 11$

c) $3.2 + x = 4.6$

d) $x - \dfrac{2}{7} = 5$

e) $x - 2 = -7$

$x - 2 + 2 = -7 + 2$

$x = -5$

f) $x + 7 = 4$

g) $2.7 + x = -6.1$

h) $x + \dfrac{5}{8} = \dfrac{1}{2}$

3. Check your answers to Question 2 by replacing x with your answer. Is the equation true?

a) $8 - 3 = 5$ ✓

b)

c)

d)

e)

f)

g)

h)

REMINDER: $(+) \times (+) = +$ $(+) \times (-) = -$ $(-) \times (+) = -$ $(-) \times (-) = +$

$(+) \div (+) = +$ $(+) \div (-) = -$ $(-) \div (+) = -$ $(-) \div (-) = +$

---

4. Multiply or divide.

a) $3 \times (-2) = \underline{\quad}$

b) $8 \div (-4) = \underline{\quad}$

c) $(-9) \times (-3) = \underline{\quad}$

d) $(-9) \div (-3) = \underline{\quad}$

e) $-9 \times 5 = \underline{\quad}$

f) $-20 \div 5 = \underline{\quad}$

Bonus ▶ $(-18) \div (-4.5) = \underline{\quad\quad}$

5. Get back to *x* on the left side. Do the same thing to the right side to solve the equation.

    a) $3x = 12$ b) $\dfrac{x}{-4} = 20$ c) $0.8x = -4.8$ d) $\dfrac{x}{-5} = -6$

Sometimes you need two steps to solve an equation.

Step 1: Do the same thing to both sides to get the variable term by itself.

Step 2: Do the same thing to both sides to make the coefficient equal to 1.

Example: Solve $-2x + 3 = 11$.

Subtract 3 from both sides:

$$-2x + 3 - 3 = 11 - 3$$
$$-2x = 8$$

Divide both sides by -2:

$$-2x \div (-2) = 8 \div (-2)$$
$$x = -4$$

---

6. Do the same operation to both sides to get the variable term by itself. Do not solve.

    a) $2x - 5 = 17$ b) $3x + 4 = 13$ c) $-3x + 14 = -10$

    $2x - 5 + 5 = 17 + 5$

        $2x = 22$

    d) $7x - 13 = 22$ e) $-x - 3 = -10$ f) $2x + 5 = -3$

7. Solve the equation. Check your answer in your notebook by substituting your answer for *x* in the original equation.

    a) $3x - 5 = 16$ b) $2x - 9 = -5$ c) $-3x + 5 = -19$

    $3x - 5 + 5 = 16 + 5$

        $3x = 21$

      $3x \div 3 = 21 \div 3$

          $x = 7$

    d) $\dfrac{x}{5} + 4 = 3$ e) $\dfrac{x}{-3} + 8 = 3$ f) $-\dfrac{x}{2} - 3 = 7$

8. Abdul can rent skis for $3 an hour. A ski ticket costs $20 for the day.

    a) How much does it cost to ski for 3 hours?

    b) How many hours can Abdul ski if he has $41?

9. Use the distributive property to rewrite the equation without brackets.

a) $2(x + 3) = 16$

   $2x + 6 = 16$

b) $3(5 - x) = 12$

c) $-3(x + 2) = 6$

d) $-2(x - 3) = 8$

e) $-4(3 - x) = 20$

f) $-2(-5x + 4) = 11$

10. Use cross multiplication to rewrite the equation without fractions.

a) $\dfrac{2x - 3}{5} = 4$

b) $\dfrac{2(4x + 1)}{3} = 14$

c) $\dfrac{x + 8}{3} = \dfrac{2}{-5}$

d) $\dfrac{2x - 5}{-3} = \dfrac{-4}{7}$

e) $\dfrac{5 - 3x}{3} = \dfrac{-1}{4}$

Bonus ▶ $\dfrac{2}{3}(5 - 3x) = 8$

11. Rewrite the equation if you need to. Then solve the equation.

a) $4(x - 7) = 12$

b) $\dfrac{x + 4}{5} = 4$

c) $-3(x + 4) = 15$

d) $22 = 3x + 4$

e) $15 + 2x = 9$

f) $3(x - 5) = 12$

g) $-3(x + 2) = 6$

h) $\dfrac{x + 11}{2} = 3$

i) $\dfrac{x}{2} + 7 = 4$

j) $\dfrac{x}{2} + 3 = 9$

k) $\dfrac{x - 5}{4} = 1$

l) $-5x + 2 = -13$

12. Solve $3(x + 4) = 21$ two ways. Make sure you get the same answer both ways.

a) Start by expanding $3(x + 4)$.

b) Start by dividing both sides of the equation by 3.

59. Solving Two-Step Equations—A Shortcut

Here are two ways to solve $x + 3 = 7$.

Method 1: Use preserving equality.

$$x + 3 = 7$$
$$x + 3 - 3 = 7 - 3$$
$$\text{So } x = 7 - 3$$

Method 2: Use logic.

$x + 3 = 7$ means you have to add 3 to x to get 7.

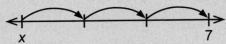

So you have to subtract 3 from 7 to get x.

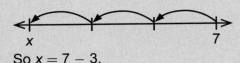

So $x = 7 - 3$.

In both methods, the 3 moved to the other side and was subtracted instead of added.

1. To get the variable term by itself, move the constant term to the right side. Remember to change addition to subtraction.

   a) $x + 7 = 15$

   $$x = 15 - 7$$

   b) $3x + 4 = 19$

   c) $-x + 9 = 12$

   d) $2x + 10 = 4$

   e) $7 + 4x = 15$

   f) $7 + 2x = 3$

   g) $5 - 3x = 8$

   $$-3x = 8 - 5$$

   h) $7 - 2x = 3$

   i) $0.8 - 2.6x = -7$

You can solve $x - 3 = 7$ two ways.

Method 1: Use preserving equality.

$$x - 3 = 7$$
$$x - 3 + 3 = 7 + 3$$
$$\text{So } x = 7 + 3.$$

Method 2: Use logic.

$x - 3 = 7$ means you have to subtract 3 from x to get 7. So you have to add 3 to 7 to get x.

So $x = 7 + 3$.

In both ways, the 3 moved to the other side and was added instead of subtracted.

2. To get the variable term by itself, move the constant term to the right side. Remember to change subtraction to addition.

   a) $2x - 5 = 11$

   $$2x = 11 + 5$$

   b) $x - 7 = 11$

   c) $4x - 5 = 6$

   d) $3x - 4 = -10$

   e) $0.6x - 5 = 1$

   f) $-4 + 3x = 8$

You can move any term to the other side of an equation. Just change addition to subtraction and subtraction to addition. Example:

You have to subtract 2 from A to get B.

$$5x - 3x + 4x - \mathbf{2} = 7 + 3 - 8$$

A   B

So you have to add 2 to B to get A.

$$5x - 3x + 4x = 7 + 3 - 8 + \mathbf{2}$$

A   B

3. Move all the variable terms to the left side and all the constant terms to the right side.
Do not solve the equation.

a) $3x + 5 - x = 7$

$3x - x = 7 - 5$

b) $8x + 4 = 3x - 11$

$8x - 3x = -11 - 4$

c) $7 - 4x = x - 3$

d) $2x + 8 - 5x = 14$

e) $9x - 5 = 11x + 5$

f) $2x - 8 = 5x + 1$

An equation with all the variable terms on one side and all the constant terms on the other side is easy to solve.

Step 1: Simplify the side with the variable terms and evaluate the side with the constant terms.

Step 2: Divide both sides by the coefficient of the variable.

Example: $3x - x - 4x = 7 - 9 + 8$

$$-2x = 6$$

$$-2x \div (-2) = 6 \div (-2)$$

$$x = -3$$

4. Solve the equation.

a) $x + 6x - 4x = 10 - 1$

$3x = 9$

$x = 3$

b) $7x - 5x = 7 - 1$

c) $9x - 2x + x = 5 + 7 - 2 + 6$

d) $5x - 4x + x = -8 - (-2)$

e) $3x - 7x = 2 - (-10)$

f) $2x - 4x - x = 7 - 5 - 8$

g) $7x - 9x = 11 - 5$

h) $2x - 4x - x = 7 - 13$

i) $x - 5x = -1 - 2 - 8 + 4 - 1$

5. Rewrite the equation without brackets. Then move all the variable terms to the left side and all the constant terms to the right side. Do not solve the equation.

a) $3(x - 5) = 13 - x$

$3x - 15 = 13 - x$

$3x + x = 13 + 15$

b) $2(x + 3) = x - 5$

c) $2(7 - 2x) = 5(x - 8)$

d) $3(5 - x) - 2 = 7(x - 1)$

e) $4(9 - x) = 3x - 13$

f) $2(3x + 4) = 4(5 - 3x)$

To solve an equation:

Step 1: Rewrite the equation without brackets if you need to.

Step 2: Move all the variable terms to one side and all the constant terms to the other side.

Step 3: Simplify both sides of the equation.

Step 4: Divide by the coefficient of x.

You just solved for x!

Example: $3(2x - 3) + 4 = -2(x + 4) - 5$

$6x - 9 + 4 = -2x - 8 - 5$

$6x + 2x = 9 - 4 - 8 - 5$

$8x = -8$

$x = -1$

---

6. Solve the equation.

a) $-x - 3 = x - 9$

b) $3x - 17 = 5x - 9$

c) $3(x + 5) = x + 7$

d) $3(5 - x) = 2(4 - 5x)$

e) $6 + \dfrac{2}{3}x = 11 - x$

f) $\dfrac{3}{5} + 5x = \dfrac{7}{5} - 3x$

g) $3(x + 4) - 10 = 2(x - 2)$

h) $2(3x + 7) = 5(9 - 2x) + 1$

i) $3(2x - 5) = 2x + 9$

7. Check your answers to Question 6 by substituting your answer into the original equation.

60. Solving Problems Algebraically

When you use a variable to solve a word problem, you are solving it **algebraically**. Always start by letting the variable represent what you want to know.

1. What would you use x to represent?

a) Clara has 5 times as many apples as Matt. Clara has 35 apples. How many apples does Matt have?

Let x be ___the number of apples that Matt has___.

b) Randi needs to save $60. She makes $12 an hour. How many hours does she need to work?

Let x be _____.

c) Tim works 15 hours and makes $10 an hour. How much money does he make altogether?

Let x be _____.

d) Tess is three times as old as Sal. Sal is four years younger than Mona. Tess is 15 years old. How old is Mona?

Let x be _____.

e) Pedro bought 250 pencils for 15¢ each. He sells them for 25¢ each. How much profit does he make?

Let x be _____.

f) May buys pencils for 15¢ each. She sells them for 25¢ each. She wants her profit to be $30. How many pencils should she buy?

Let x be _____.

2. Three children have 30 apples altogether. Nick has x apples. Complete the table and write the equation.

a)
	Expression
Lynn has 2 more apples than Nick.	$x + 2$
Josh has twice as many apples as Nick.	$2x$

Equation:

$$\underbrace{x}_{\text{Nick's apples}} + \underbrace{x + 2}_{\text{Lynn's apples}} + \underbrace{2x = 30}_{\text{Josh's apples}}$$

b)
	Expression
Lynn has 4 times as many apples as Nick.	
Josh has 6 more apples than Nick.	

Equation:

3. Solve the equations in Question 2. How many apples does each child have?

4. a) Three children have 40 apples altogether. Jen has x apples. Complete the table.

		Expression
i)	Ross has twice as many apples as Jen.	$2x$
	Sun has 5 more apples than Ross.	$2x + 5$

		Expression
ii)	Ross has 5 times as many apples as Jen.	
	Sun has 4 fewer apples than Ross.	

		Expression
iii)	Ross has 2 more apples than Jen.	
	Sun has 6 fewer apples than Ross.	

		Expression
iv)	Ross has 5 fewer apples than Jen.	
	Sun has 5 times as many apples as Ross.	

b) Write an equation you could solve to find x.

i) $x + 2x + 2x + 5 = 40$

ii) _____

iii) _____

iv) _____

c) Solve your equations from part b). How many apples does each child have? Check your answer.

5. a) Raj has 30 apples. Zara has x apples. Complete the table.

		Expression
i)	Sam has 4 times as many apples as Zara.	$4x$
	Raj has 2 more apples than Sam.	$4x + 2$

		Expression
ii)	Sam has 5 times as many apples as Zara.	
	Raj has 5 fewer apples than Sam.	

		Expression
iii)	Sam has 2 more apples than Zara.	
	Raj has 3 fewer apples than Sam.	

		Expression
iv)	Sam has 2 fewer apples than Zara.	
	Raj has 5 times as many apples as Sam.	

b) Use an equation to find x. How many apples does each child have?

6. Nancy has twice as many apples as Jay. Jay has 3 more apples than Ava. Nancy has 22 apples. How many apples does Ava have?

7. Bo has 8 times as many apples as Amy. Bo has 7 more apples than Don. Don has 41 apples. How many apples does Amy have?

8. Kami buys pens for $4 each and sells them for $4.50 each. How many pens does she need to sell to make a profit of $50?